That
Patchwork
Place®

In The Beginning

Seattle, Washington USA

Sharon Evans Yenter

CREDITS

Photography .... Doug Plager
Photo Stylist .... Nancy J. Martin
Illustration and Graphics .... Stephanie Benson
Cover Design......................... Judy Petry
Text Design .... Stephanie Benson
Editor .... Barbara Weiland
Copy Editor .... Miriam Bulmer

In the Beginning ©
© 1992 by Sharon Yenter
That Patchwork Place, Inc., PO Box 118,
Bothell, WA 98041-0118

Printed in the British Crown Colony of Hong Kong
97 96 95 94 93 92   6 5 4 3

Yenter, Sharon Evans,
     In the beginning / Sharon Evans Yenter.
          p.   cm. — (Quilt shop series)
     ISBN 1-56477-005-2 :
          1. Patchwork—Patterns. 2. Quilting—Patterns.
     I. Title. II. Series.
TT835.Y46 1992
746.46—dc20   91-45195
                                          CIP

DEDICATION

To my mother, Florence O'Connor Evans, who successfully raised a family of six children and continues to help each of us spiritually, emotionally, and financially. She's the lovely lady you'll meet working at the store on Sundays (for free). Thanks, Mom.

ACKNOWLEDGMENTS

With thanks and appreciation . . .

To my husband, Bill, who's helpful, supportive, and puts up with a lot!

To my sons, Jason and Ben, who have grown up with In the Beginning and now work there happily. Thanks, guys!

To our co-managers, Jackie Quinn and Kathleen Grady, who have spent many long days in the wrong pair of shoes and remained gracious and friendly.

To our hard-working staff, past and present, who have made the store a success.

To Janet Kime, for her many hours of help in putting this project together.

To Nancy J. Martin, president of That Patchwork Place, Inc., for having the creativity to think we could magically turn a store into a book.

To our customers, those loyal, talented, and wonderful folks who appreciate the things we do to make the store special.

To the talented women at Pickity Patch Florist in Seattle for the floral arrangements in the photographs.

To Sara Evans, Pat Yenter, and Florence Evans for the use of their prized accessories featured in the photos.

Just as In the Beginning is a success because of the contributions of many people, this book benefits from the ideas, projects, and expertise of many friends who have been exceedingly helpful over the years. Special thanks to Marsha McCloskey, Lorraine Torrence, Leslee Shepler, Nancyann Twelker, Gretchen Engle, Virginia Lauth, Jackie Quinn, Michele Quinn, and Judy Sogn for their writing and stitching skills and their contributions to this book.

Contents

Introduction

When Nancy Martin, president of That Patchwork Place, Inc., first approached me about doing a book, I was in the middle of writing my shop's class schedule and newsletter. This is a shop owner's most dreaded task, and I'm afraid I was stressed out and a little grumpy. I probably said something like, "Oh, sure, who needs sleep? If God had wanted all of us to sleep, he wouldn't have invented coffee!"

But as I hung up the phone, I started thinking about the projects, classes, and contests we've had at In the Beginning. I remembered the forty-five newsletters I'd done over the years. One book seemed like a snap. Will I never learn?

I left my two college-going sons and a very capable staff to run the store and headed home. I hadn't worked at home for a long time. Would I remember my favorite corners to stash the heaps of fabric projects? Jessamyn West once stated, "When I'm writing a book, I never get out of bed because if I get out of bed I always find something that needs dusting." After the sewing machine slid off my pillow for the tenth time, I vowed I would ignore the mess, leave my bed, and get to work. Why be a perfect housekeeper now? I was an author!

My family and friends were duly impressed with my literary career and commented on how successful I was. Smiling, I accepted their admiration. I've fooled them for fifteen years—would I be discovered now? As the book progressed, it became apparent that the projects included were the work of many people, and the secret was out. Every successful business person up to and including the President of the United States knows how it works: surround yourself with talented people, encourage and allow their creativity, and they'll make you look good.

In the Beginning has been a team effort. We've had a great time and loved every minute. Each day has been an adventure, with new projects, new people, and new ideas. I now treasure my newsletters as a diary of the store; going back over the years and recalling people and events has been a delight. I've extracted some of our most successful patterns and happenings for this book. Try our projects and come into the store and share your results with us when you're in the Pacific Northwest. We'd love to see you. We're located at 8201 Lake City Way NE in Seattle.

Fabric and Color

The fabrics in the stores today are glorious and bountiful. Quilters have more choices than ever before. Companies are manufacturing hundreds of new designs every season. While this might seem like the happiest circumstance ever, it presents a dilemma for shop owners.

Just as a budget is a fact of life for your personal finances, it is also necessary to the success of a retail business. If we reorder last season's fabrics, we will not have enough dollars to buy the new designs. It's no fun to have to tell a customer that we can't order the extra yard (or quarter or half yard) that it will take to finish a quilt or special project. Even if we agree to place a special order, it may be six weeks to three months before the fabric arrives.

The solution to this problem is to either buy enough fabric or substitute another piece if you come up short. Keep this in mind when purchasing fabric for the projects in this book. I've allowed generous yardage, so you may have a small amount left over to add to your fabric collection.

The fabrics I have used are all 100% cotton. Most of the projects use either chintz or Liberty of London™ Tana™ Lawn. These are fabrics we carry in our inventory, and I like the different looks they impart. You can substitute other medium to large florals if you like.

Chintz is usually seen in home-decorating projects these days, but it was considered the prestige fabric for quilts in the 1800s. Our chintz is mainly Cyrus Clark, Waverly, or Concord. It is 54" wide, so you will have some extra fabric with which to work. Chintz is lovely for home-decorating projects because it is heavier than most quiltmaking fabrics. (Coordinate your window treatments for a beautiful, professional look.) Despite its weight, I have hand quilted chintz and it worked well; it also machine quilts beautifully. Washing chintz removes much of the glazed finish, so if you want to maintain the polished look, I recommend dry cleaning. I suggest that chintz not be prewashed, although you will want to preshrink the other fabrics you will be using with the chintz.

A selection of lovely chintzes

It is a treat to work with fine lawn, probably the finest quality cotton fabric you will ever find. It is quite pricey, so you might want to use it in small amounts, combined with other fabrics. The colorations are exquisite, and many screens are used to achieve the vibrant designs. Liberty Tana Lawn is 36" wide, so calculate your yardages accordingly.

Many of the projects in this book utilize fabrics with low-contrast colorations. Most quilters are familiar with using light, medium, and dark values to achieve areas of high contrast. The low-contrast technique is appropriate for large florals, where the seams between individual fabric pieces tend to disappear, so that areas of the quilt look like large bouquets. Often, the pieced pattern is almost lost, as in Rescued Star (page 18) and Hidden Star (page 69). Many chintz quilts from the early to mid-1800s are examples of low-contrast coloration. You will notice it particularly in antique Welsh or English quilts.

To achieve this effect, you must combine several medium-value, small- to large-scale floral prints with a small amount of light-value fabric. The result will be a soft Victorian-era look.

Another color technique used in this book combines many fabrics of light, medium, and dark values that wash together so that no one print is distinct.

In the late 1800s, impressionists, such as Claude Monet, Auguste Renoir, Georges Seurat, and Mary Cassatt, developed a new style of painting, exploring color and light in ways that captured their feelings about nature and life. They were colorists, and one of their most important discoveries was the broken-color technique. When different colors are applied to the canvas very close to each other, the viewer's eye mixes them and reads them as a color totally different from its components.

English artist Deirdre Amsden was the first to apply this technique to quilts, and variations have followed. In her colorwash series, colors shade together and no one print is outstanding. (This technique is featured in the Colorwash with Arrows quilt by Lorraine Torrence on page 42.) Deirdre used Liberty Tana Lawn, but small to medium florals from fabric manufacturers, such as Hoffman, Gutcheon, Concord, or V.I.P., can also be used. It is important to select multicolor prints rather than two-color fabrics.

A group of Liberty of London™ *Tana*™ *Lawns, showing the range of colorations available*

General Directions

Before you start the projects in this book, turn to the Glossary which begins on page 74. Many general instructions and techniques not fully covered in the individual project directions are presented there. It's always wise to review these instructions and pick up some new tips.

I surely could have benefited from the paragraph on batting when I made my first quilt. My batt was so thick, the quilt looked like a life raft!

Some pattern pieces are printed on the pullout pattern section stapled into the center of the book. Open the staples to remove the pages; close the staples again to keep your book intact. Glue a large manila envelope to the inside back cover of the book for pattern storage.

Trace all other templates onto tracing paper, available at many quilt stores. This allows you to make templates without cutting into your book and destroying the instructions or templates on the reverse side of the pages.

All seams are ¼" unless otherwise noted.

The patchwork templates in this book are marked with grain-line arrows to show you how they should be placed on the fabric. The arrows should be aligned with the straight grain of the fabric. The straight grain runs parallel to the selvage and has no stretch. If the piece of fabric you are working with does not have a selvage, stretch it in several directions to find the cross grain, which has a little stretch. The bias grain stretches a lot, and the lengthwise grain hardly stretches at all.

Cooking over a Hot Sewing Machine

My husband Bill's astrological sign is Cancer. Maybe that's why his home is his castle, and if its condition resembles something out of fifteenth-century England that has been ignored for hundreds of years, he's oblivious to the fact and loves it anyway.

When we entertain, it's a day filled with frenzy as we clear out my dining/sewing room. (Does this sound familiar to anyone?) I figure the best way to make guests forget their surroundings is to give them lots of good food, so I cheat and use shortcuts. I have a few well-used recipes that work every time, and they're real man-pleasers. (Sexist, but true.) Whether you work outside the home or are a stay-at-homemaker, there are never enough sewing hours in a day. With these recipes, your friends will think you've been slaving in the kitchen all day when you've really been cooking over a hot sewing machine. Don't forget the flowers and candles if you're into gracious living.

COMPANY CHICKEN

Really quick and easy.
3 whole chicken breasts (divided into 6 halves)
1 t. seasoning salt
1½ c. long-grain white rice
1 4-oz. can mushrooms with liquid
1 10-oz. can cream of mushroom soup
1 10-oz. can cream of celery soup
1 envelope dry onion soup mix
1 t. savory
2 c. chicken broth

Preheat oven to 350°F. Sprinkle chicken with seasoning salt. Grease 3-quart casserole well and spread rice over bottom. Layer with mushrooms, then chicken. Mix undiluted soups with savory and dry soup mix. Pour over mixture in casserole. Pour broth around sides to moisten rice. Cover with foil and bake for 1½ hours. Serves 4 to 6.

WINE CAKE

Try this on a busy sewing day—the subtle flavor will make them think that you've been baking all day.
1 box yellow cake mix
1 3.4-oz. box vanilla instant pudding
¼ t. nutmeg
¼ c. water
¾ c. cooking oil
¾ c. cream sherry wine (It must be cream sherry.)
4 eggs

Preheat oven to 350°F. Beat all ingredients together for 5 minutes. Pour into a greased Bundt or angel food cake pan. Bake for 45 minutes. Cool in the pan 10 minutes, then turn out onto a plate and sift powdered sugar over the top.

Victorian House

In the Beginning . . . It all started with this Victorian House. Actually, it was quite a bit more complicated, but this is the pattern I first taught at the store. When my children were young, in the early 1970s, I created items to sell in boutiques and at street fairs. The Victorian House was by far my best seller.

One day I was sitting in the refreshing Seattle rain, listening to the umpteenth customer say to a friend, "Twenty-five dollars! Gosh, Mabel, my grandmother makes dozens just like these for nothing. How does she have the nerve to charge twenty-five dollars!" Suddenly a gust of wind came around the corner and capsized my entire booth. My handwork flew up like kites in the sloppy spring air, making a colorful procession in the sky. It was then that I began to think seriously of another line of work.

My mother and sister had started a store to sell gifts, cards, and dollhouse miniatures, and they called it "In the Beginning." They had an extra 240 square feet of pie-shaped balcony and offered it to me. I knew the frustration I had in finding fabrics and the feeling of accomplishment I received from my sewing, so I called some fabric distributors and jumped right in. Needless to say, vendors were unimpressed with my operation, wanted cash only, and assumed I would last maybe six months.

Finished size: 17" x 24"

MATERIALS:
44"-WIDE FABRIC

⅔ yd. medium-weight nonwoven interfacing, such as Pellon

½ yd. sky fabric

¾ yd. print for backing, trees, and bush

¼ yd. pieces (or scraps) for the roof, house, steps, chimney, door, windows, outer window trim, and posts

¼ yd. each of three fabrics for the landscape and foreground

18" x 24" piece of thin polyester batting

7" of lace

3 cabone rings, ¾"-diameter (small plastic drapery rings)

The variety of chintz fabrics in this wall hanging gives it a Victorian look. You can use calicoes or solid colors for a different look.

It's best to use heavier fabrics for the house and roof because you will be sewing the multiple-layer windows onto them. Most bottom-weight dress fabrics are fine. If you want to use a lightweight fabric, first fuse it to another fabric with Wonder-Under™ or another fusible product following manufacturer's directions.

The three landscape fabrics should blend into each other. Choose a coordinating print for the trees, bush, and backing. Remember, the Victorians used many prints together to achieve their charming look.

I've used hand-dyed fabric for the sky. Some shops carry hand-dyed fabrics, and some manufactured fabrics really look like sky. You might even try painting a sky fabric yourself.

CUTTING
Use pattern pieces on pullout pattern insert.

1. Cut an 18" x 24" piece of medium-weight interfacing.
2. Cut a 13" x 18" piece of sky fabric.
3. From the backing fabric, cut a 22" x 28" piece.
4. Cut out the paper patterns on the pullout sheet. Following the instructions on the patterns, cut out all fabric pieces. Note the ¾"-wide seam allowance on some ground pieces.

ASSEMBLY

1. Use the satin stitch on your sewing machine to appliqué the pieces. Set your machine as directed in your sewing-machine manual. As you will be sewing three layers (fabric, batting, and interfacing) most of the time, do not make your satin stitch too closely spaced.

   Practice the satin stitch on a scrap of fabric. If your fabric pulls or puckers or the stitches seem too tight, you may have to decrease the stitch tension by turning the tension knob to a lower number. This gives a looser upper-thread tension.

2. Lay the batting on top of the interfacing, and then the sky piece over the batting. Arrange pieces A, B, C, D, and E on the batting, overlapping each as indicated on the pattern pieces. Pin in place.

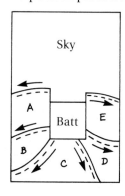

Victorian House, 17" x 24"

3. Machine appliqué the ground pieces, stitching in the directions indicated by the arrows. Set aside.

4. Arrange windows P, I, U, and door M on the house and roof. Dotted lines on the house and roof show the correct placement of pieces. Pin in place, or use a glue stick or a fusible web, such as Wonder-Under. Machine stitch each piece in place around the edge with a narrow zigzag stitch.

5. Place door window N and inside curved windows V on the house and zigzag around. Mark the curved lines on the windows with a fine-line permanent marker or pencil, then stitch with a very narrow satin stitch.

    The windows are the most time-consuming part of the project. You might try stitching a few curves on a scrap of fabric for practice before you add the details to the windows.

6. Position roof K on the sky 3" down from the top and 5¾" in from the left side. Pin in place.

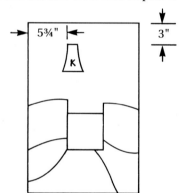

7. Slit house piece F as indicated on the pattern piece. Slide roof J through the slit and behind house tower to overlap allowance.

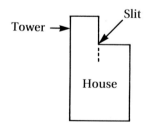

8. Arrange the rest of the pieces on the background, except the porch roof L, porch posts O, chimney Q, and small bush R. Place trees and bush under house to the lap allowances. The lattice piece overlaps the house and the steps overlap the front door. Pin in place.

9. Pin the lace onto the roof tops. Tuck the raw end of the lace on roof J under roof K.

10. Sew around the trees S and T with a satin stitch.

11. Stitch pieces down, following the diagram, and beginning with the right roof. Start at the top of the roof lace and sew down the roof. Continue down to the bottom of the house lattice. Stitch horizontally across the bottom of the lattice, the top of the lattice, the bottom of roof J, and across the bottom of the lace on roof J.

12. Flip up roof piece K and sew the house on both sides of the tower from X to W in the direction of the arrows.

13. Mark the step lines with a pencil. Lap the steps over the door and sew horizontally. Sew top of steps, pencil lines, and bottom of steps.

14. Starting at the lace of roof K, stitch all around roof.

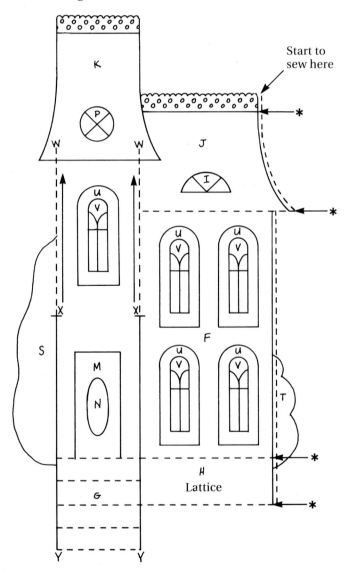

* Sew across these pieces horizontally

15. Do not stitch between X and Y; the posts will cover this. Position posts O with roof L removed. Sew around posts. Place roof over posts and sew all around.
16. Tuck chimney under lace and stitch around it. Draw a curly line for the chimney smoke and sew with a medium-width zigzag stitch.
17. Pin bush R in place and stitch around.
18. Use a yardstick to even up the edges of the piece; mark and trim off the excess.
19. Center the house on the wrong side of the backing fabric. Allow about 2" all around for the backing to be folded around to the front.
20. Press under ¼" all around the backing fabric. Then fold the backing fabric around to the front and pin through all layers.
21. Cut small triangles off each corner, then fold under to make a 45° angle and pin.

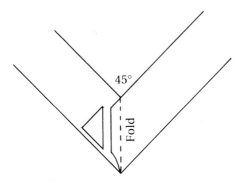

22. Hand stitch around the frame that the backing has created, or machine stitch with a decorative stitch. Slipstitch corners.
23. Sew a cabone ring to the top back of the wall hanging at the center and at each corner.

The following thoughts were contributed by staff members during a wine-cake testing session. (See page 7 for the recipe.)

The Good Customer Handbook

Our favorite customers always compliment us on a new hairdo, dress, or jewelry. They admire our children's prom and graduation pictures, ooh and ahh at snapshots of our babies or grandkids, take our suggestions, and admire our choices.

Our favorite customers are fabriholics and, unlike our husbands and friends, understand how we can spend all of our paychecks at the store.

Our favorite customers, when queried by their husbands about all the checks written to In the Beginning, reply that they've bought a Bible or made a charitable donation.

Our very favorite customers bring us cakes or cookies. Dorothy Arbuckle, a customer without peer, has even been known to bring fresh crab off her beach.

Star Sampler: Pattern of the Month

I opened my section of the store in 1977, and at the end of six months, Mom and sister Sara moved to another store in Tacoma, Washington. I inherited 1800 square feet of space, a two-year lease, and a name that sounded like a maternity shop or a drug rehabilitation program. I was across the street from a mortuary, so the store became known as "In the Beginning, across from In the End." It was now "Mortgage Bill's Castle" time, and we were on our way.

Marsha McCloskey, one of our first teachers, offered our Beginning Sampler Quilt class. In 1980, we started handing out her Pattern-of-the-Month block series. Each month, Marsha drafts a traditional pattern in an 8" block, and we print the templates and instructions, along with store information, and distribute the handout to customers. We still do this and have many customers who collect the patterns religiously.

Included here are six star patterns that were handed out over the years, along with a lattice set designed by Marsha. You can substitute any 8" blocks of your own and use the set and border. The quilt pictured was created with many Liberty of London prints, but could be duplicated with any small to medium low-contrast prints.

Quilt size: 33" x 42"
Block size: 8"

MATERIALS:
36"- OR 44"-WIDE FABRIC

8 fat quarters or 2 yds. total assorted prints
¾ yd. for border
1½ yds. for backing
½ yd. for binding

CUTTING

Use templates on page 15.
1. From each of the 8 fat quarters, cut 6 squares, 2" x 2", for a total of 48 squares
2. From each of 6 fat quarters, cut 4 strips, 2" x 8½". From each of the other 2 fat quarters, cut 5 strips, 2" x 8½", for a total of 34 strips. Set these pieces aside for the lattices and Fourpatch setting blocks.
3. From the border fabric, cut 4 strips, each 4" x 42".
4. From the remaining fat quarter fabrics, cut the pieces for the 6 star designs as shown in the diagrams. As

shown in the photo, this is a scrappy quilt made of medium- to low-contrast prints. In some blocks, the star almost disappears. As you cut the pieces for each star, refer to the block illustration for color placement.

STAR BLOCKS

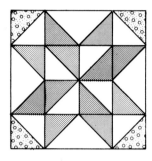 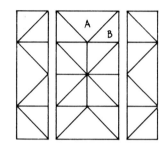

1. *Star Puzzle:*

Cut 4 of Template A.   Cut 8 of Template B.

Cut 12 of Template B.

Cut 4 of Template B.

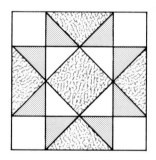 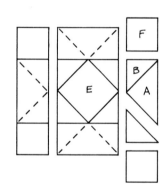

2. *Variable Star:*

Cut 4 of Template A.   Cut 1 of Template E.

Cut 8 of Template B.   Cut 4 of Template F.

Cut 4 of Template B.

Star Sampler (Pattern of the Month), 33" x 42", by Marsha McCloskey, Sharon Yenter, Gretchen Engle, Michele Quinn

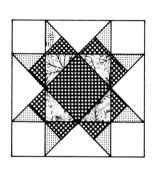

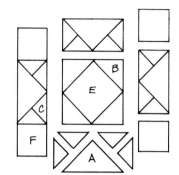

 Cut 1 of Template F.   Cut 4 of Template F.

Cut 4 of Template G.

3. Missouri Star:

Cut 4 of Template A.   Cut 8 of Template C.

Cut 4 of Template B.   Cut 1 of Template E.

Cut 8 of Template C.   Cut 4 of Template F.

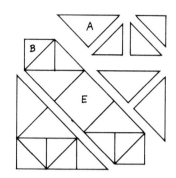

6. Castles in Spain:

Cut 4 of Template A.   Cut 4 of Template B.

Cut 4 of Template A.   Cut 4 of Template B.

Cut 4 of Template B.   Cut 1 of Template E.

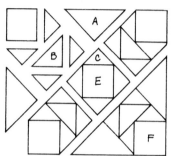

4. Broken Star:

Cut 4 of Template A.   Cut 8 of Template C.

Cut 4 of Template B.   Cut 4 of Template F.

Cut 4 of Template C.   Cut 4 of Template F.

Cut 8 of Template C.

ASSEMBLY

1. Make each of the 6 blocks, following the piecing diagrams. See Glossary (page 74) for machine piecing techniques.
2. Piece 12 Fourpatch blocks and 17 lattice sections.
3. Arrange the pieced 8" star blocks with the strips and squares, following the quilt photograph on page 13. It should look scrappy.
4. Assemble 3 rows, each containing 2 star blocks and 3 lattice sections. Assemble 4 sashing rows, each containing 3 Fourpatch blocks and 2 lattice sections. Assemble quilt, alternating sashing rows with block rows. Refer to the quilt photo on page 13.

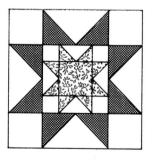

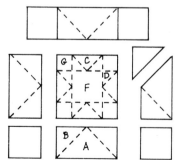

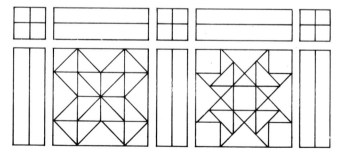

5. Rising Star:

Cut 4 of Template A.   Cut 4 of Template C.

Cut 8 of Template B.   Cut 8 of Template D.

5. Add 4"-wide border strips to the sides of the quilt and trim. Add border strips to the top and bottom.
6. Add batting and backing, and quilt or tie. Bind the edges with bias binding. See Glossary, which begins on page 74, for finishing techniques.

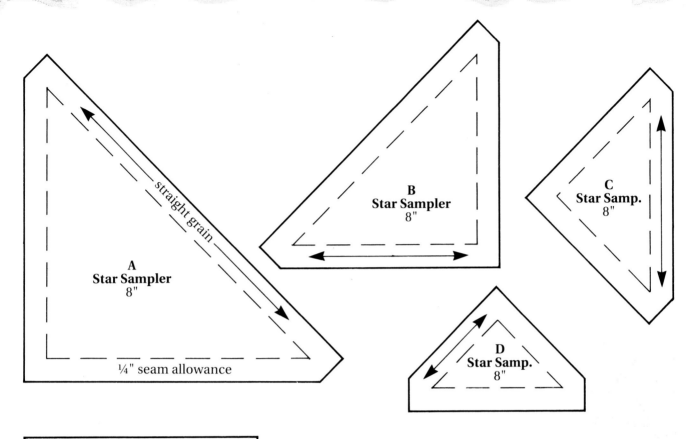

A
Star Sampler
8"

straight grain

¼" seam allowance

B
Star Sampler
8"

C
Star Samp.
8"

D
Star Samp.
8"

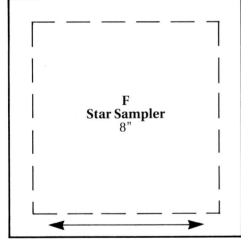

F
Star Sampler
8"

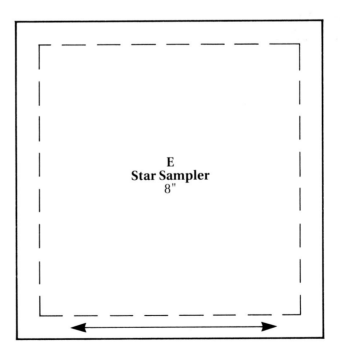

E
Star Sampler
8"

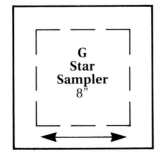

G
Star
Sampler
8"

Constellation Star and Rescued Star

One of my favorite pastimes is looking for antique quilts. I love to rescue even the ratty ones and take them home. Someone spent a lot of time thinking, talking, and daydreaming over each quilt, and I think these artifacts of their lives deserve respect.

I especially enjoy the "break-out" quilts, wild and wondrous creations made by adventurous women in a rigid society. I have several of the "Oh, look what Aunt Maude gave us, dear" variety that must have lain in drawers for a hundred years, because they are in mint condition. The eccentricity of the Aunt Maudes of the world live on in these quilts, and I love the charm and the "I-can-do-it" attitude they evoke.

In the early years of the store, I was forced to sell many antique quilt treasures to pay the overhead. One day, Marsha McCloskey was working while I was out of the store. A decorator with her client in tow came in and started rummaging through our antique quilts. She decided on a wonderful old quilt that had thirty blocks. As they brought it to the counter, the decorator was rhapsodizing on how terrific all thirty pillows would look around the client's house.

Marsha, not normally an aggressive person, was incensed. She refused to sell the quilt, and they left the store in a huff. I'm sure I lost two customers, but I've managed to keep the quilt to this day. It's a reminder to me that many things in this world are more important than money, and the landlord will always wait another day.

These instructions are for creating a replica of the original antique quilt, the traditional name of which is Constellation Star. Instructions follow for a six-block chintz version I call Rescued Star.

Constellation Star

Quilt size: 72" x 85"
Block size: 10"

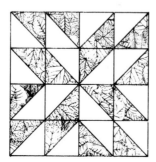

MATERIALS: 44"-WIDE FABRIC

3 yds. for border and lattice strips
2¾ yds. each of 2 contrasting fabrics, if all blocks are identical; or ⅛ yd. each of 2 fabrics for each of 30 blocks
5 yds. for backing
¾ yd. for binding

CUTTING

Use Template A on page 18.

1. For each of 30 star blocks, cut 16 of Template A in one fabric, and 16 of Template A in a contrasting fabric. If all of the blocks are identical, cut 480 of Template A of one fabric, and 480 of Template A of the contrasting fabric.
2. Cut 25 lattice strips, each 3½" x 10½". Cut 4 lattice strips, each 3½" x 75½".
3. Cut 2 border strips, each 5½" x 62½", and 2 border strips, each 5½" x 85½".

ASSEMBLY

1. Piece 30 blocks, using 32 triangles in each, following the piecing diagram.

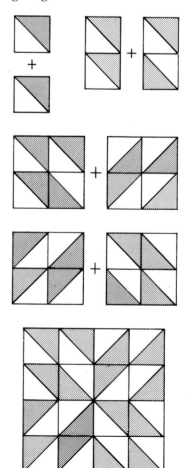

Constellation Star, 72" x 85", anonymous quiltmaker, circa 1910

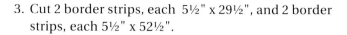

2. Assemble blocks and short lattice strips into vertical rows. Join rows with long lattice strips.

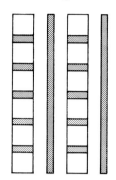

3. Attach the top and bottom borders, and then the two long side borders.
4. Add batting and backing, and quilt or tie. Bind edges with bias binding. See Glossary, which begins on page 74, for finishing techniques.

Rescued Star

Quilt size: 39" x 52"
Block size: 10"

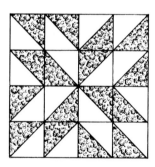

3. Cut 2 border strips, each 5½" x 29½", and 2 border strips, each 5½" x 52½".

ASSEMBLY

1. Following the piecing diagram for Constellation Star on page 19, assemble 6 blocks.
2. Sew blocks and short lattice strips into vertical rows as shown. Join the 2 rows with the center lattice strip.

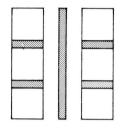

3. Add the 23½" lattice strips to the top and bottom, then the 42½" lattice strips to the sides.

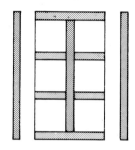

4. Attach the top and bottom borders, and then the side borders.
5. Add batting and backing, and quilt or tie. Bind edges with bias binding. See Glossary, which begins on page 74, for finishing techniques.

MATERIALS:
44"- OR 54"-WIDE FABRIC

⅛ yd. each of 2 fabrics for each block, 6 blocks total
1¼ yds. for lattice
1⅝ yds. decorator stripe for border
1⅝ yds. for backing
½ yd. for binding

CUTTING

Use template A on this page.

1. For each of 6 star blocks, cut 16 of Template A from one fabric, and 16 of Template A from a contrasting fabric.
2. Cut 4 lattice strips, each 3½" x 10½", 1 center lattice strip, 2½" x 36½", 2 top and bottom lattice strips, each 3½" x 23½", and 2 side lattice strips, each 3½" x 42½".

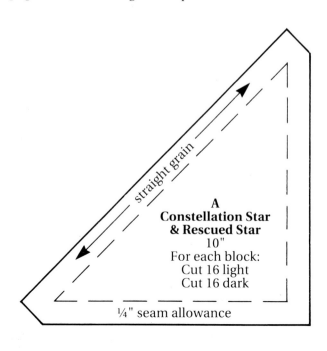

straight grain

A
Constellation Star & Rescued Star
10"
For each block:
Cut 16 light
Cut 16 dark

¼" seam allowance

Rescued Star, 39" x 52", by Gretchen Engle, Sharon Yenter, and Virginia Lauth

Church Window

Seventeen years ago, quick sewing techniques fascinated me because I was producing fabric items for resale. Seminole techniques were being discovered by non-Native Americans, and I spent months experimenting in a flurry of enthusiasm.

Recently, however, I have come to enjoy the relaxation of hand sewing. I really enjoy sewing fabrics onto paper patches as I ride in a car or watch television. It is so mindless, it is restful, and there are many creative possibilities.

You can spend months putting this top together by hand, and when you are almost finished, you can dust off your sewing machine and strip piece the border in an evening, using Seminole techniques.

Hexagons have been identified with English patchwork since the mid-1700s. In this variation, Church Window, the sides are elongated. This particular pattern was featured in *Godey's Lady's Book* in the 1880s, and that pattern may have been the inspiration for this quilt. The top was pieced by Anna Hayes Miller, niece of President Rutherford B. Hayes, while she journeyed by ship around the Horn on her way to a new home in Tacoma, Washington. I wonder what hopes and expectations went into this quilt.

Quilt size: 42½" x 55½"

MATERIALS:
44"-WIDE FABRIC

1½ yds. total assorted fabrics for hexagons
1 yd. muslin for squares and strip-pieced border
½ yd. print #1 for strip-pieced border
½ yd. print #2 for strip-pieced border
¾ yd. striped fabric for inner border
1½ yds. for backing
½ yd. for binding

CUTTING

Use templates on page 23.

1. Trace the hexagon Template A onto an 8½" x 11" piece of paper and continue to trace hexagons until sheet is filled. Repeat with Templates B and C. Take the sheets to a print shop and have the hexagon sheet copied enough times to make 260 hexagons. Make a total of 228 of Template B and 62 of Template C. Cut out all paper shapes. In addition, cut 4 paper pieces using Template D.

2. Cut 260 of Template A from the hexagon fabrics, adding ¼"-wide seam allowances all around.

3. Cut 228 of Template B, 62 of Template C, and 4 of Template D from the muslin.

4. For the corner stars, cut 16 of Template G from print #1, and 16 of Template G from print #2. Cut 16 of Template F and 16 of Template E from muslin.

5. For the striped inner border, cut enough 2"-wide strips to piece 2 pieces each 46" long, and 2 pieces each 48" long.

6. For the strip-pieced border, cut 8 muslin strips, each 2" x 44" (cut selvage to selvage). Cut 4 strips of print #1 and 4 strips of print #2, each 3" x 44".

ASSEMBLY

1. Pin each paper template to a fabric patch. Pin on the underside, so your thread won't catch on the pin.

2. Starting on one of the long sides of the hexagon, turn the ¼" seam allowance over onto the paper template and baste to the paper. Paper-piece all pieces cut from Templates B, C, and D.

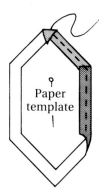

3. When all of the hexagons are paper-pieced, pin them to a piece of fleece or flannel or work on a design wall and move them around until you find an arrangement you like.

4. To join the hexagons, match two right sides together and sew them together with an overcasting stitch, being careful not to catch the paper.

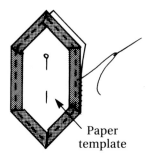

Church Window, 42½" x 55½", by Anna Hayes Miller, circa 1885, quilted in 1983 by Virginia R. Koucky

5. Attach a square (B) to the top of each pair of hexagons.

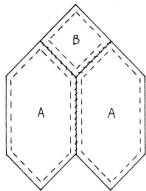

6. Join these pairs of hexagons into 13 rows of 20 hexagons each, adding the remaining squares (B) and triangles (C and D). Or, work in sections and then join the sections, if you find that more manageable. Refer to the quilt photo on page 21.

7. When the quilt top is completely assembled, press carefully. Remove the basting stitches, and pull out all the paper pieces.

8. Piece the striped 2"-wide strips to make 2 that are 46" long and 2 that are 48" long. Add the striped inner border to the 4 sides of the quilt, mitering the corners. (See page 74.)

9. The outer border can be speed-pieced from the 2"-wide strips of muslin and the 3"-wide strips of prints #1 and #2. Before you begin, draw a pencil line down the exact center of the wrong side of the #1 strips. (Check first to be sure the pencil mark does not show through on the right side.)

10. Sew the strips into 4 units of muslin / print #1 / print #2 / muslin. Press.

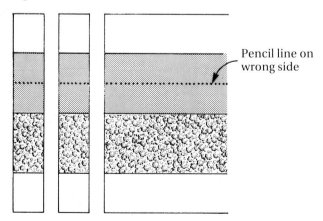

Pencil line on wrong side

11. Crosscut the units into 1½"-wide pieces. You should get about 29 from each unit, for a total of 116.

12. Sew the pieces together in pairs, offsetting as shown. Match the muslin-print #1 seam to the line drawn on the wrong side of all the #1's.

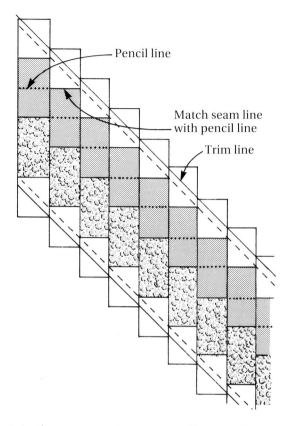

Pencil line

Match seam line with pencil line

Trim line

13. Join the pairs, continuing to offset, until you have 1 long strip.

14. Cut the strip into 2 pieces 40" long and 2 pieces 48" long. Set aside.

15. Using paper templates, baste the diamonds for the corner stars, leaving the tails unturned. Baste the background squares and rectangles.

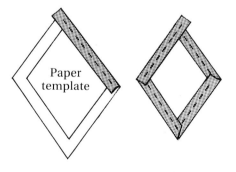

Paper template

16. Sew the diamonds together in pairs, starting at the largest angle and sewing with an overcasting stitch to the points.

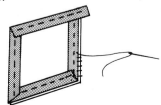

Sew the pairs together to make the 2 halves of the star, then join the 2 halves.

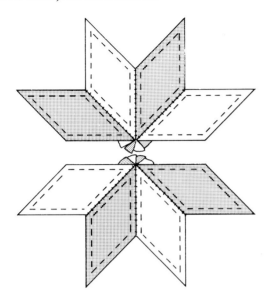

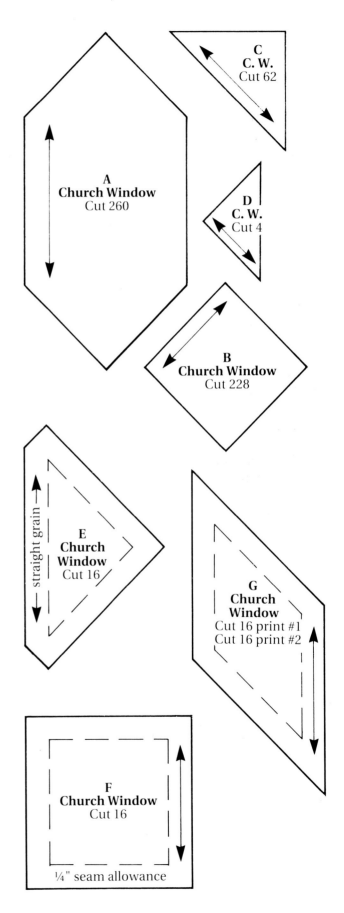

17. Attach the background squares (F) and triangles (E) between the star points to finish each star as shown.

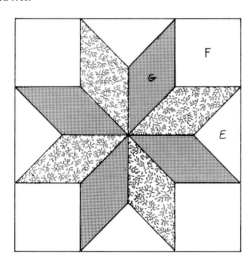

18. Sew the star blocks to both ends of the shorter strip-pieced borders.
19. Add the long strip-pieced borders to the sides of the quilt. Add the border-with-star pieces to the top and bottom of the quilt.
20. Add batting and backing, and quilt or tie. Bind edges with bias binding. See Glossary for finishing techniques.

Irish Garden Chain

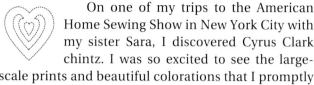

BAG LADIES IN NEW YORK

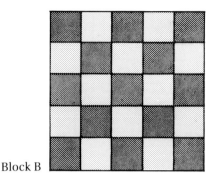

On one of my trips to the American Home Sewing Show in New York City with my sister Sara, I discovered Cyrus Clark chintz. I was so excited to see the large-scale prints and beautiful colorations that I promptly placed a large order. The salesman dropped some samples in a large shopping bag and I was on my way.

As a confirmed fabriholic, when I'm not at a fabric show purchasing for the store, I'm searching for fabric shops to buy material to add to my ever-growing personal collection. At the end of a rainy afternoon of successfully scouring Manhattan for fabric, we decided to stop and eat. Several years earlier, we had been to New York and enjoyed a lovely meal at the RCA Building. We decided to find the restaurant again and rode the elevator to what we thought was the correct floor. As we exited the elevator, we spotted a restaurant straight ahead. The handsome blond host surveyed our brimming shopping bags, dripping hair, and damp clothing, smiled menacingly, and said, "We try not to make this look like a picnic in Alaska."

Undeterred, we followed him into a spectacular empty dining room, glowing with chandeliers, with large windows draped in velvet and satin. We knew this was not the place! Our bags of fabric would not be comfortable here! We thanked him, made a hasty retreat, and spent a few hours in a corner of the lobby, fabric at our sides, watching men in tuxedos and women in designer gowns enter the renowned Rainbow Room, Manhattan's most elegant restaurant.

Jackie Quinn made this Irish Chain quilt because we found the chintz fabric at the show in March, over Saint Patrick's Day. She calls it Irish Garden Chain. I call it "Welcome to the Rainbow Room!"

Quilt size: 59" x 69"
Block size: 10"

Block B

MATERIALS:
44"- OR 54"-WIDE FABRIC

2 yds. chintz (C)

1½ yds. blue (B)

1 yd. rose (R)

1 yd. for inner border and binding

4 yds. for outer border and backing

Note: If you wish to center a floral motif in each block, as shown in the color photo, purchase extra chintz yardage.

CUTTING

Use templates on page 26.

1. Cut 15 pieces of chintz (C), each 6½" x 10½".
2. From remaining chintz (C), cut 30 of Template B and 60 of Template A.
3. From blue (B), cut 240 of Template A.
4. From rose (R), cut 135 of Template A.
5. For the inner border, cut 8 pieces, each 2" x 36".
6. For the outer border, cut 2 pieces, each 3½" x 72", and 2 pieces, each 3½" x 62".

ASSEMBLY

1. Piece 15 of block A and 15 of block B, following the block diagrams. See Glossary (page 75) for chain-piecing instructions.

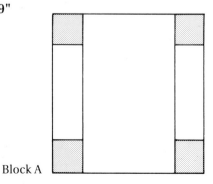

Block A

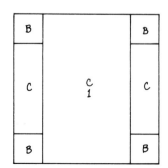

Block A

Block B

Irish Garden Chain, 59" x 69", by Jackie Quinn and Michelle Quinn

2. Sew the blocks together in 5 vertical rows of 6 blocks each. Start 3 rows with an A block and 2 rows with a B block. Sew accurate ¼"-wide seams, so the individual blocks cannot be discerned and an allover chain pattern develops. Join rows to complete quilt center, referring to the quilt photo on page 25.

3. Join the inner border pieces together to form 4 strips, each 72" long.

4. Sew the inner borders to the outer borders. Press. Sew the completed border strips to the sides (72") and top and bottom (62") of the quilt. Miter the corners as shown on page 74 of the Glossary.

5. Add batting and backing, and quilt or tie. Bind edges with bias binding. See Glossary for finishing techniques.

IDEA FOR THE DAY . . .

"Two dollars' worth of creativity, please!"

Run to your favorite fabric store and buy a quarter yard of fabric. It will lift your spirits and get you thinking positively. Where else can you find such inexpensive therapy?

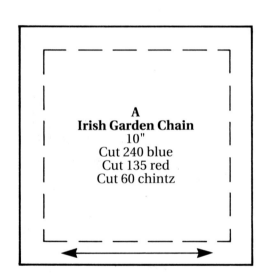

A
Irish Garden Chain
10"
Cut 240 blue
Cut 135 red
Cut 60 chintz

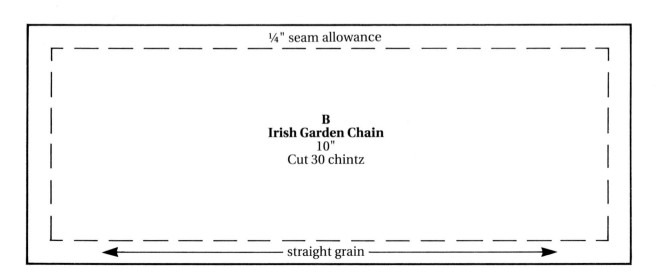

¼" seam allowance

B
Irish Garden Chain
10"
Cut 30 chintz

straight grain

A day at In the Beginning with staff members ready to help. Pictured from left: Leah Nelson, Nancy Forrest, Chris Curtis, Betty Eckstein, Janice Amiel-Grawl, Jackie Quinn, Kathie Koepsell, Bev Murrish, Kathleen Grady, Virginia Beresford.

Rose Wreath

Receiving this quilt was one of the happiest Christmas events of my life. Twenty years earlier our oldest son, Jason, was born two weeks early on Christmas Eve. I'm not sure which was the bigger surprise but I was thrilled with each.

The store staff had been planning the quilt for months and they were sure I suspected. They knew I collect red-and-green quilts and decided on a Rose of Sharon variation. It was a teary presentation when I opened the large gift-wrapped box. I was overwhelmed by the thoughtfulness and lovely workmanship that had gone into the project.

The quilt hangs on our living-room wall each Christmas. I scatter others from my collection around the house. One holiday season, we had an open house for my husband's business associates. As one couple departed, I heard the wife exclaim to her husband, "Their house must have bad walls. It's very peculiar how she has blankets covering all of them."

Quilt size: 63½" x 63½"
Block size: 15"

MATERIALS:
44"-WIDE FABRIC

2½ yds. white for background
2 yds. dark green for leaves, outer border, sashing, and stems
½ yd. solid red for roses and inner border
½ yd. red print for roses
Scraps of light red and white print for rose centers
¼ yd. light green for leaves and stems
Scraps of yellow for buds
3⅞ yds. for backing
½ yd. for binding
Red embroidery floss
Green embroidery floss

CUTTING

Use templates on pullout pattern insert.

1. Cut 9 squares, 16" x 16", from background fabric.
2. For outer border, cut 4 strips, each 3½" x 65", from the dark green. Cut these pieces parallel to the selvages, *before* you cut any other pieces from the dark green.
3. For the appliqués, cut:
     36 of Template 1 from dark green
     36 of Template 2 from light green
     36 bias strips, each 1" x 6", from dark green
     36 bias strips, each 1" x 4½", from light green
     36 of Template 2 from red
     36 of Template 3 from the red print
     36 of Template 4 from the red print scraps
     18 of Template 5 from the yellow scraps

   Note: Be sure to add ¼"-wide seam allowances as you cut each appliqué piece. The seam allowance is already included in the bias-strip measurements.
4. For the setting blocks, cut 80 of Template A from the background and 64 of Template A from dark green.
5. For sashing, cut 24 strips, each 1½" x 15½", from background and 48 strips, each 1½" x 15½", from dark green.
6. For inner border, cut ¾"-wide strips of solid red and piece to make a total length of 240".

ASSEMBLY

1. Make a full-size pattern of the Rose Wreath appliqué block, using the pattern on the pullout pattern insert. Trace the design onto each of the 9 background squares.
2. Prepare the appliqué pieces and bias strips as described for paper-patch appliqué in the Glossary on pages 77–78.
3. Appliqué the bias stems to each block, tucking the end of the light stem under the dark stem. Appliqué the remaining pieces in numerical order (2, 3, 4, 5). Add embroidered embellishments as shown in the appliqué pattern. Press each block and trim to 15½" x 15½", making sure the appliquéd design is centered in the block.
4. From the small squares (A) of background and dark green, assemble 16 Ninepatch blocks.

Rose Wreath, 63½" x 63½", by Mary Hickey, Gretchen Engle, Jackie Quinn, Judy Pollard, Evelyn Kramer, Tricia Lund, Judy Olson, Kathleen Grady, Judy Knickerbocker, Mary Davies

5. Assemble 24 sashing strips from the background and dark green strips.

6. Assemble 3 rows, each containing 3 appliquéd blocks and 4 sashing strips. Assemble 4 sashing rows, each containing 3 sashing strips and 4 Ninepatch blocks.

7. Assemble quilt, alternating sashing rows with rows of appliquéd blocks and lattice. Begin and end with a sashing row. Refer to the photo on page 29.
8. Add a red inner border strip to the sides of the quilt, then to the top and bottom.
9. Add dark green border strips to the sides of the quilt, then to the top and bottom.
10. Add batting and backing. Quilt the blocks in diagonal lines and use the quilting design included on the pullout pattern insert to quilt the borders. Bind edges with bias binding. See Glossary for finishing techniques.

My Legacy

FROM OUR NEWSLETTER

"My Legacy" appeared nearly thirteen years ago in our newsletter. The author is unknown, but the situation is familiar!

◇ ◇ ◇

Being of a sweet and generous nature, it has always been my desire to spare my husband as much trauma as possible. I have, therefore, never consulted with him about the fabric I buy. I feel that he should be grateful that I am a fabriholic instead of an alcoholic and be willing to indulge my small passion as long as he isn't aware of the actual expenditure represented by my growing horde.

One day recently, however, I was struck by the realization that I could die, and what would happen to my fabric? My children are old enough to take care of themselves, but my fabric is helpless.

I buy fabric for the sheer pleasure of owning it. It is stashed in every available drawer, on shelves, in boxes, on the end of the cutting table (greatly reducing its use), and under the bed, until we are in danger of having to use a ladder to get onto the mattress.

It rests, carefully folded, labeled, wrapped in clear plastic so that the color and texture are clearly visible. I unwrap a piece occasionally, hold it up to the light,

enjoy the hand, visualize how it might look made up, measure it again to ascertain that it has not diminished, then I carefully refold it, place it in the plastic, and return it to its storage place. I rarely find a pattern worthy of my prizes, so that when I really want to make up something, I have to go out and buy fabric into which I can bear to cut.

The confirmed fabriholic really doesn't want to make quilts or clothing from her treasures, she just enjoys having them. The true connoisseur collects only natural fibers. Synthetics do not tempt the heart of the purist. They are changing so fast that whatever you buy this year will be old hat next year. Not so with natural fibers. Good silks, woolens, cottons, and linens become more rare and costly.

Becoming a grandmother shocked me into admitting that I am not immortal and will eventually leave this vale of needles and pins and will have to leave my store behind, although I am certain that if the angels saw my fabric they would find a way for me to bring it along to stitch up into Heavenly Robes. I began to feel like a miser with coins stashed in the mattress. Someone would have to be told about it. I waited until my husband was peacefully engaged in his favorite pastime, and broached the subject.

Centennial Rose
Quilt Photo: page 33

There are so many deserving causes in the world, and groups are always needing money. Over the years, the staff members of In the Beginning have made quilts for each other, new babies, and several charitable causes. In 1984, one of our quilts raised $1500 for Northwest Second Harvest, a Seattle food bank.

I have fond memories of the old Mickey Rooney/Judy Garland movies when he'd say, "Hey, gang, we've got a barn, let's put on a show!" As a tap-school drop-out at the age of six, dancing was beyond my capabilities, and I could only dream in envy.

In 1989, Nancyann Twelker curated a show of quilts historically important to the state of Washington. The show, called "Women and Their Quilts," toured the state as part of our centennial celebration. Money to insure the quilts and pay travel expenses was in short supply. It was as easy as saying, "Hey, gang, we've got the fabric, let's make a quilt!" The In the Beginning staff pitched in and produced a Centennial Rose quilt, which we raffled off, raising $2000 for the touring quilt show!

Centennial Rose, based on a design by Bryce Hamilton, is easy to appliqué and very elegant.

Quilt size: 88½" x 102"
Block size: 19½"

MATERIALS:
54"-WIDE FABRIC
3½ yds. solid white for background
3 yds. blue chintz print for outer flower petals (Template 1) and borders
½ yd. light pink print for large flower center (Template 2)
½ yd. blue print for middle flower center (Template 3)
¼ yd. dark pink print for small flower centers (Template 4)
¾ yd. green solid for leaves

1 yd. pink-and-white stripe for inner border
5⅞ yds. 44"-wide fabric for backing
¾ yd. for binding

CUTTING
Use templates on pullout pattern insert.
1. From background, cut 9 squares, each 20" x 20", and 1 piece, 25" x 59", for the pillow section of the quilt top.

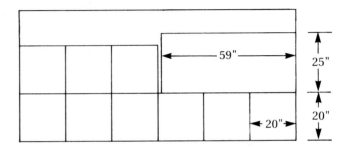

2. Cutting parallel to the selvage of the chintz print, cut 2 side border strips, each 11½" x 102", and 1 bottom border strip, 11½" x 88½".
3. For the appliqués, cut:
   40 of Template 1 from the remaining chintz print
   10 of Template 2 from the light pink print
   16 of Template 3 from the blue print
   16 of Template 4 from the dark pink print
   120 of Template 5 and 2 bias strips, each 1½" x 18", from the solid green
   Note: Be sure to add ¼"-wide seam allowances as you cut each appliqué piece. Seam allowances are already included in the measurements for the bias strips.
4. For the inner borders, cut 7 strips, each 4½" wide, from the pink-and-white stripe. Cut strips across the width of the fabric (crosswise grain).

ASSEMBLY
1. Center and trace the Centennial Rose appliqué design on each of the 9 background squares, using the full-size pattern on the pullout insert in the center of this book.
2. Prepare the appliqué pieces as described for paper-patch appliqué in the Glossary (page 77).
3. Complete each block, positioning and appliquéing the pieces in numerical order. Press completed blocks carefully.
4. Assemble 3 rows of 3 blocks each. Stitch rows together. Referring to the photograph of the quilt on page 33, center an appliqué 3 over each seam

intersection. Stitch in place. Add an appliqué 4 to the center of each one. Stitch in place.

5. Referring to the quilt photo, position the remaining chintz petals in the center of the pillow section; pin.

6. Prepare 2 bias strips, each 18" long, following the directions for appliqué stems in the Glossary (page 78). Tuck one end of each strip under opposite petals. Curve strips as desired and pin in place.

7. Stitch petals and stems in place.

8. Position and appliqué remaining pieces as shown in the quilt photo. Carefully press the completed pillow section.

9. Sew 2 of the 4½"-wide striped strips together, end to end, to make an inner border for one side. Repeat for the other side border.

10. Cut 1 of the remaining 3 striped strips in half crosswise and sew each half to 1 of the other strips, to make the top and bottom inner borders.

11. Cut 1 of the shorter striped border strips to 58½" and sew this to the top edge of the quilt. Sew the 24¾" x 58½" pillow piece to the top of the border strip.

12. Cut the other short striped border to 65" and sew it to the bottom edge of the quilt, making sure that 3½" extends on each side for mitering.

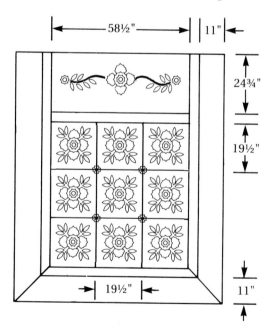

13. Trim the striped side borders to 91½". Do one side at a time, being sure that the strips match and create a chevron when mitered, before you cut the strip. Sew the strip to the side, mitering the corner as shown in the Glossary (page 74). Repeat on the remaining side.

14. Sew the longer outer borders to the sides of the quilt and the shorter border to the bottom edge, leaving the excess extending from both bottom corners. Miter the corners as shown in the Glossary.

15. Add batting and backing. Quilt in the ditch around each appliqué. Quilt cables in the striped inner borders and quilt the background in diagonal lines 1½" apart. Bind edges with bias binding. See the Glossary for finishing techniques.

Centennial Rose Quilt, 88½" x 102", by Leah Nelson, Bev Murrish, Betty Eckstein, Sharon Yenter, Virginia Beresford, Chris Curtis, Leslee Shepler, Kathleen Grady, Jackie Quinn. Assembled by Gretchen Engle, quilted by Virginia Lauth.

Skagit Beauties Block

In 1980, we held our first quilt-block contest. We distributed packets of material to exert some control over the colors, but entrants were allowed to add additional fabrics and select their own block patterns. The blocks were displayed in the store, and customers voted for their personal favorites. Thirteen winners were selected, and their blocks were assembled into a quilt top that the store then had hand quilted. After the quilt was completed, we had a drawing, and one of the thirteen won the quilt. The first quilt was very brown and rust, as I recall, and some of the workmanship in the blocks was primitive but charming.

We continued to have a quilt-block contest every year until 1989. Our all-time most lucky participant was Janice Richards, who won the first two contest quilts. On the evening of the drawing for the third quilt, Janice called and declined winning a third time if her name was drawn. I thanked her, thinking it pretty unlikely, and proceeded to draw her name out of the basket!

As the years went by, the quality of the blocks became quite extraordinary. Our last contest quilt was the 1989 Centennial Quilt, made to honor Washington State's 100th anniversary. The quilt is spectacular and has won Viewers' Choice awards at several quilt shows around the state. It traveled throughout Washington and was a fitting representative of the talent and ingenuity of Washington quilters.

All of the blocks are original, or original interpretations of traditional blocks. Patterns are not available, but Judy Sogn agreed to share her Skagit Beauties pattern, which was a favorite with viewers. It represents the beautiful tulips that bloom in profusion in the Skagit Valley each spring. Make a block for a pillow top or wall hanging, or make several to use in a quilt.

Block size: 15"

MATERIALS:
44"- OR 54"-WIDE FABRIC

¼ yd. green print for leaves (should contrast with green for stems)
¼ yd. green print for stems
Scraps of gold
Scraps of light rose
Scraps of dark rose
½ yd. background

CUTTING

Use templates on pullout pattern insert.

Note: Be sure to add seam allowances as you cut each appliqué piece.

For each block, cut:

    8 of Template 1 and 8 of Template 6 from the green print for leaves

    8 bias strips (B), ¾" x 3", from the green print for stems. See page 78 of the Glossary for bias-strip stem technique

    8 of Template 3 from gold

    8 of Template 4 from light rose

    8 of Template 5 from dark rose

    1 background square, 16" x 16"

ASSEMBLY

1. Draw a full-size pattern of the appliqué block, using the pattern on the pullout pattern insert, and trace onto the background square.
2. Prepare the appliqué pieces and bias strips as described for paper-patch appliqué in the Glossary (page 77). Appliqué the pieces in numerical order.
3. Press block thoroughly and trim to 15½" x 15½", centering the appliquéd design in the block.

Skagit Beauty block, 15", by Judy Sogn

Quilt Block Contest—1989 Washington Centennial Quilt, 90" x 90". From the top, left to right: Bonnie Mitchell, Kathleen O'Brien, Judy Pollard, Mignonette Wright, Cheryl Campbell, Judy Sogn, Sue Linker, Pat Magaret, Janet Kime, Frieda Martinis, Louise Rose, Joan Hanson, Betty Charette. Assembled by Marsha McCloskey, quilted by Andrea Balosky.

Feathered Star, 82" x 101", by Gisella Thwaites. The pattern for the feathered stars is in the book Christmas Quilts *by Marsha McCloskey. The pattern for the pieced border is in the book* Back to Square One *by Nancy J. Martin.*

Liberty of London Accessories and Quilts

Many of the projects in this book feature fabrics from Liberty of London. Their Tana Lawn is unique in coloration and quality. In 1989, I won a trip to England, compliments of Creative Product News, a wholesale trade publication. One of the highlights of my visit was a shopping trip at the Liberty of London store in midtown London. It's a large store, housed in an older building reminiscent of a department store of the early 1900s—all dark wood and balconies. It's a treasure trove of Oriental rugs, gift items, clothing, a lovely tea room, and—best of all—their wonderful fabric.

My son Jason was studying in London at the time, and I had arranged to meet him in the evening. As I was happily sorting through stacks of fabrics, I felt someone looking at me. I glanced up to see Jason and a friend standing nearby. "We were on our way to a matinee, but I knew I'd find you here, so we came in," he said. A city of millions and he knew where to find me!

While at Liberty, I spied a beautiful quilt hanging over a balcony three floors above. I rushed up the stairs and discovered the exquisite quilt shown in the photo at left. It was created by Gisela Thwaites of Newport Pagnell, U.K. Gisela used muslin and Liberty of London Tana Lawn, which gives it a mellow, antique look. Much to my surprise, I discovered that it had been made using a Feathered Star design by Marsha McCloskey, previously published in *Christmas Quilts*, and a pieced border design by Nancy Martin, previously published in *Back to Square One*.

The quilt now resides in Seattle, where it has been admired by visitors to our store. It has also appeared at numerous quilt shows and is a wonderful representative of all the talented British quilters.

Quilt-Block Keeper

Leslee Shepler has been teaching at the store for almost fifteen years. She has a talent for adapting "old-time" accessories into useful and lovely items for today. This quilt-block keeper is based on one originally made in the 1930s by Leslee's grandmother. Leslee has updated it and thinks it's a great way to show off a special fabric.

Roll your quilt blocks around the tube and wrap the keeper around them, to avoid creasing, soiling, or even losing blocks. Your friends will admire your cleverness. Leslee warns that this is no pretty excuse to avoid finishing your quilt. You are not allowed to store quilt squares forever!

Quilt Block Keeper, 20" x 32", and Pin-Stuck Cushion, 3" x 5", by Leslee Shepler

Project size: 20" x 32"

MATERIALS:
36"- OR 44"-WIDE FABRIC

¾ yd. cover fabric
¾ yd. fine white cotton for lining
½ yd. coordinating stripe or print for bias binding
20" cardboard tube, from a roll of wrapping paper
Fiberfill or batting scraps to stuff the tube
Potpourri (optional)
Lace doily (optional)
1 yd. 1"-wide ribbon
1 button, 1" in diameter
Tacky craft glue
2 rubber bands

CUTTING

1. Cut a 20" x 32" piece of the cover fabric. Also cut 2 circles, each 4" in diameter.
2. Cut a 20" x 32" piece of the lining fabric.
3. Cut and prepare 3 yards of 2"-wide bias, following the directions on page 76 of the Glossary. Fold in half, lengthwise, wrong sides together, and press, being careful not to stretch the fabric.

ASSEMBLY

1. Stuff the cardboard tube with fiberfill or batting scraps. If you wish, add potpourri alternately with the fiberfill to make a hidden sachet.
2. Apply tacky glue to the outer ½" of the ends of the cardboard tube and center a circle of fabric over each end. Smooth over the glue and hold with rubber bands until dry.

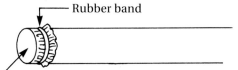

Rubber band

Fabric circle

3. Place the outer fabric and lining fabric, wrong sides together. Round the corners of one end if desired. (Round one corner, then fold piece in half and cut the other corner to match. You can use a small bowl or saucer as a template for this, if you like.)

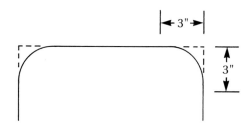

4. Machine baste lining to outer fabric.
5. Stitch bias strip to the outside along unfinished edge of block keeper, leaving one short edge (the one you didn't round) unbound. Refer to the directions for bias binding on page 76 in the Glossary. Be careful not to stretch the bias strip as you go around the corners. Turn bias to inside and hand stitch over the seam line. Press.

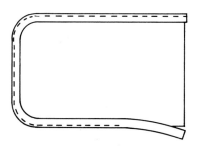

6. Roll the raw edges of the fabric onto the tube. You may want to use a small amount of tacky glue to anchor it. Roll the fabric around the tube 1½ times, to hide the raw edges. Whipstitch by hand to hold the fabric firmly on the tube.
7. If desired, hand stitch a lace doily onto the outside of the block keeper.
8. Fold the ribbon in half and place the center close to the bottom edge of the keeper. Stitch firmly by hand or machine.

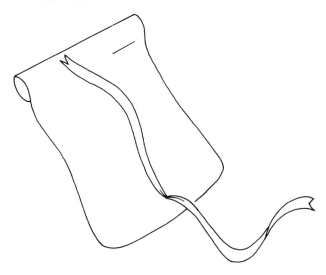

9. To make a pretty fabric rosette, cut a 2¼" x 9" bias strip from a scrap of contrasting fabric. Stitch, right sides together, along the short edges, forming a ring.

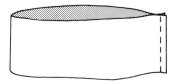

Fold the ring in half, right side out, with raw edges matching. Run a basting stitch around the raw edges and pull to gather. Tack. Sew in place on top of the ribbon, then sew the button in the center.

Pin-Stuck Cushion

In the seventeenth, eighteenth, and nineteenth centuries, small cushions were embellished with pin messages as tokens of friendship or love. Every trousseau and layette included these special mementos.

Leslee Shepler designed this small project (photo on page 37) using sequin pins, which are short straight pins available in many quilt and craft stores.

Project size: 3¾" x 6¼"

MATERIALS:
36"- OR 44"-WIDE FABRIC
Scrap of white cotton for cushion center
Scraps of print for cushion border and back
Water-soluble marking pen
1 yd. narrow piping (optional)
Polyester fiberfill
Buttons and ribbons (optional)
Sequin pins

CUTTING
Use template on this page.
1. From the white scrap, cut 1 of Template A for the cushion center.
2. From the print, cut 4 of Template A for the cushion border and 1 piece, 4¼" x 6¾", for the cushion back.

ASSEMBLY
1. Tape the center rectangle onto a flat surface and write a name or simple message, using the water-soluble marking pen.
2. Add the top and bottom border strips, then the sides. Press, being careful not to press over the pen markings.

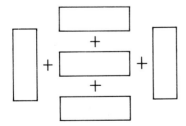

3. If desired, baste piping around the outside of the piece with raw edges even. Use a zipper foot to stitch close to the piping.
4. Place backing on front, right sides together, and stitch together inside basting line. Leave a 2" opening along the bottom edge.
5. Clip corners; turn right side out through opening.
6. Stuff firmly with fiberfill and hand stitch the opening closed.
7. Decorate with buttons and/or ribbons, if desired.
8. Following the pen markings, stick sequin pins very close together to form letters. Remove markings with a clean, damp washcloth.

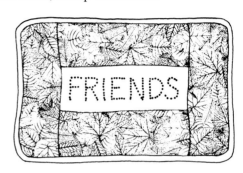

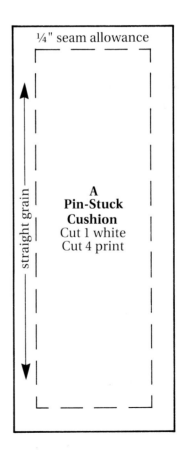

¼" seam allowance

straight grain

A
Pin-Stuck
Cushion
Cut 1 white
Cut 4 print

Strip-Quilted Stationery Holder

The fine Liberty of London Tana Lawn prints are perfect for gift accessories. One of my favorite gift ideas is this charming stationery holder designed by Nancyann Twelker. Nancyann suggests purchasing colorful notepaper and matching envelopes, available by the pound in many card shops. Choose a lovely fabric and select stationery in a coordinating color.

The cover of this stationery holder is strip quilted from scraps of Liberty prints. Strip quilting, a "quilt-as-you-go" technique, is a one-step process in which the project is quilted as you assemble it. Strips of fabric are seamed together on top of a foundation fabric and a piece of batting to make a quilted fabric. This is a quick and easy project and makes a lovely gift.

Strip-Quilted Stationery Holder, 12" x 17", by Nancyann Twelker and Gretchen Engle

Project size: 12" x 17"

MATERIALS:
36"- OR 44"-WIDE FABRIC

Scraps of 6 to 8 fabrics
½ yd. coordinating fabric for lining and pocket
½ yd. needlepunch
½ yd. coordinating print for bias binding
Thread to match lining fabric
¾ yd. ⅞"-wide ribbon

CUTTING

1. Cut fabric scraps into 12"-long strips, varying from 1¼" to 2½" wide.
2. Cut a piece of lining fabric, 12" x 17", and another, 10" x 16".
3. Cut a piece of needlepunch, 12" x 17".
4. Cut and prepare 60" of 2"-wide binding from the coordinating print as described in the Glossary on page 76. Fold in half lengthwise, wrong sides together, and press, being careful not to stretch the fabric.

ASSEMBLY

1. Place the larger piece of lining fabric, right side down, and place the needlepunch on top.
2. Place 1 strip of fabric, right side up, vertically along a short side of the foundation piece. Place another strip on top of the first strip, with right sides together and raw edges even.

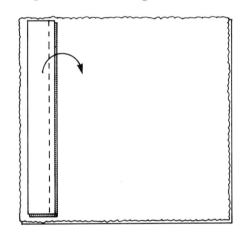

3. Stitch a ¼"-wide seam. Flip the top strip of fabric over so the right side of both strips faces up. Finger press.
4. Select another strip of fabric and place it, right side down, on top of the one just sewn. Stitch, flip, and finger press as before. Continue in this manner, placing fabrics in an arrangement that pleases you, until all the needlepunch is covered.
5. Steam press with a damp press cloth. Measure and trim the piece to 11" x 16".
6. Fold the smaller piece of lining fabric in half lengthwise to measure 5" x 16". Press.
7. Place the quilted outer fabric, right side down, on a flat surface. Place the folded 5" x 16" lining fabric

even with the bottom edge of the quilted fabric.

8. Machine stitch from A to B and from C to D, backstitching at beginning and end of stitching.

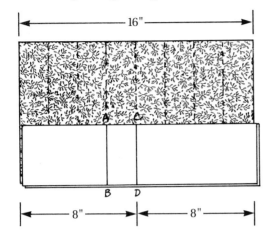

9. On the inside of the stationery holder, pin a 12" length of ribbon to each side, 6" above the bottom edge. Tuck ribbon ends in pockets or pin them to the center to keep them out of the way when binding the edges.

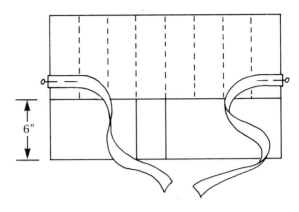

10. Bind the edges, following the instructions in the Glossary (page 76).

11. Insert stationery and a pen into the pockets. Tie the ribbons in a bow.

FROM OUR NEWSLETTER

Help for Harried Housewives

For pity's sake, don't let the laundry problem get you down. Does the very thought of doing the washing bring visions of sloshing about mournfully in huge tubs of water, or working in clouds of strong, steamy odors; of lifting pails of water; of struggling with an antiquated washer or, heaven forbid, of rubbing on a washboard; of a sketchy luncheon, a cross family, and a generally upset household?

Needlecraft Magazine, September 1938

SAY "BAG IT!" COME ON DOWN TO YOUR FAVORITE QUILT SHOP AND TAKE A CLASS!

Colorwash with Arrows
Quilt Photo: page 43

English quiltmaker Dierdre Amsden originated the concept of the Colorwash quilt by piecing together small pieces of multicolored prints, each so slightly different from the adjacent pieces that color and value seem to wash gently over the surface of the quilt, as in a watercolor painting. With Dierdre's permission, Lorraine Torrence has been offering a Colorwash class at In the Beginning in which she makes use of the beautiful Liberty of London cotton lawn prints.

In the Colorwash with Arrows project, she has added another element to the Colorwash background: multicolored inset strips ending in pieced triangles that simulate arrowheads.

The best way to make this kind of quilt is to work on a 2½' x 3' section of wall. Working at eye level, tape or tack a working surface to the wall. One option for the surface material is needlepunch, available from several manufacturers under brand names such as Pellon™ fleece or Thermo-Lam™. It is a flat polyester batting of uniform thickness, available by the yard.

Quilt size: 25½" x 32½"

MATERIALS:
36"- OR 44"-WIDE FABRIC

2 Colorwash kits from In the Beginning OR
72 multicolor, small-print fabric scraps in a wide
　　range of values and colors
11 scraps of light colored print fabric
Note: The Colorwash kit is a selection of 39 different
　　3" x 5" pieces of fabric, including many Liberty
　　of London prints. It is an economical way to
　　accumulate a wide variety of fabrics in the very
　　small amounts you need to make this quilt. For
　　mail-order information, see page 79.
¼ yd. each or scraps of 11 different solid colors
¼ yd. for inner border
¼ yd. for outer border
1 yd. for backing
½ yd. for binding

CUTTING
Use templates on page 44.
1. Cut 143 squares (Template A) from a variety of fabrics. (You may cut 2 squares from each of your 72 fabrics in the kits.)
2. From each of the 11 solid colors, cut a strip 1" x 30", a piece 1" x 2½", and 1 of Template B.

3. From 11 of your lightest fabrics, cut 1 of Template C and 1 of Template C reversed from each fabric.
4. From inner border fabric, cut 2 pieces, each 1" x 30", and 2 pieces, each 1" x 23½".
5. From outer border fabric, cut 2 pieces, each 2" x 32½", and 2 pieces, each 2" x 26".

ASSEMBLY

1. Arrange the squares on your working wall so that you have 11 squares across and 13 squares down. Place the darkest squares at the top and work down gradually to the lightest squares at the bottom. As you gradually move from dark to light, also gradually change the colors so that you create gently changing areas of color.
   Note: Sometimes it is difficult to see which of two different colors is the darker or lighter value. Try looking at your fabrics through a piece of red cellophane or transparent red plastic. You will immediately see colors as values.

   As you arrange your Colorwash background, you may find yourself wishing you had a piece of fabric just a tiny bit lighter than the one in your hand, but still the same color. Try turning the square over and using the wrong side of the fabric. Sometimes it is precisely what you need. Also, if you need a square that is dark green in the upper left corner and more pink in the lower right, locate the square carefully on your fabric so that you get the transition you need.

2. When you are satisfied with the arrangement of the squares, sew them together into rows. Then sew the rows together and press.

3. Put the Colorwash background up on your working wall and arrange the solid-colored 1"-wide strips on top of the background in a sequence that pleases you. Each vertical row of colorwashed squares should have a solid strip running down its center.

4. Remove the Colorwash background from the wall and, using a ruler, draw a pencil line down the center of the vertical row of squares at the far left. The line will be 1" in from each seam line. Cut the row in half along this line.

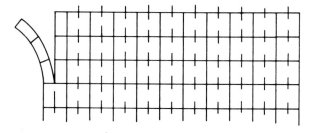

Cut apart at dotted lines

Colorwash with Arrows, 25½" x 32½", by Lorraine Torrence

5. Sew in the first long solid-colored strip where you have cut the background apart, using a ¼"-wide seam allowance. Press the seams toward the solid-colored strip.

6. Continue to cut each vertical row of background squares apart exactly down the center and insert the next solid-colored strip.

7. Arrange the 1" x 2½" pieces of solid-colored fabrics, end to end, in the same order that the colors were used in the quilt. Sew together. Sew this strip across the dark edge of the quilt, matching the colored horizontal strips to the vertical strips.

8. Sew a pair of light triangles (Template C and C reversed) to each solid-colored triangle (Template B), as shown, to make the arrowheads.

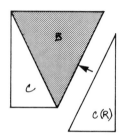

9. Sew arrowheads together in a row, matching the color order in the quilt. Sew this strip to the bottom edge of the quilt.

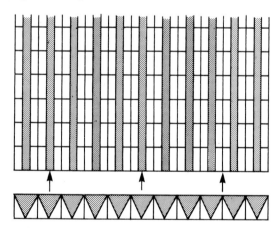

10. To construct the borders, sew each inner border strip to an outer border strip. (Sew short strips to short strips, and long to long.) Sew the border strips to the 4 sides of the quilt and miter the corners as described in the Glossary (page 74).

11. Add batting and backing, and quilt or tie. Bind edges with bias binding. See Glossary for finishing techniques.

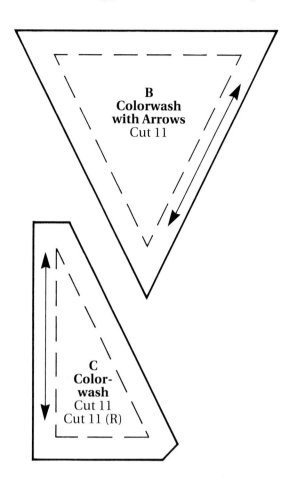

B
Colorwash
with Arrows
Cut 11

C
Color-
wash
Cut 11
Cut 11 (R)

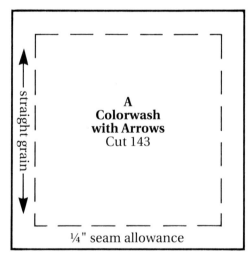

straight grain

A
Colorwash
with Arrows
Cut 143

¼" seam allowance

Ferol's Peony
Quilt Photo: page 46

Antique quilts are wonderful to study because by choice, accident, or happy circumstance, some lovely works were created. The notation on this small quilt says "Ferol Jess, age 87, 1902." The quilt was made in Pateros, Washington, but my husband, Bill, found it while scouring an antique shop in a nearby larger city.

Bill has found some wonderful and charming pieces. He had little interest in quilts when I started the store, but when your partner is obsessed with quilts, you either join in or talk to yourself a lot. He has developed a good eye for the sort of unique, quirky quilts I love.

Perhaps Ferol purchased a new sewing machine at age 87 and wanted to get her money's worth, because this piece is literally quilted to death. Each peony is carefully hand pieced, but the stems are machine topstitched. Row upon row of small machine stitches cover the quilt and carry over to the binding.

The red set blocks seem to float on this quilt because the background fabric was also used for the lattice strips. In the Ferol in London variation, I have divided the lattice strips to create a frame around the squares. I used Liberty of London Tana Lawn to create a quaint, old-world look.

Quilt size: 42" x 51"
Block size: 6"

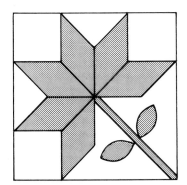

MATERIALS:
36"- OR 44"-WIDE FABRIC
1 yd. total assorted prints for peonies
1¾ yds. for background and lattice
½ yd. total assorted prints for setting squares
⅓ yd. solid green for leaves and stems
1½ yds. for backing
½ yd. for binding

CUTTING
Use templates on pages 49 and 50.
1. Cut 180 of Template A from peony fabric, or 6 for each block if you are using assorted prints.
2. Cut 90 of Template B, 30 of Template C, and 180 of Template D from background fabric.
3. Cut 20 of Template C from fabric for setting squares.
4. Cut 2 strips of solid green, each 4½" x 25", for stems.
5. Cut 60 of Template E for leaves, adding a ¼"-wide seam allowance all around.
6. For lattice strips, cut 49 of Template G from background fabric.

ASSEMBLY
1. Cut a pattern for Template F from card stock; a file folder works well. Place 1 of the 4½" x 25" strips of stem fabric on the ironing board, wrong side up. Place Template F near the end of the fabric. Press the fabric over the template to the midway point (a little over ⅛"). Fold the fabric with the template inside and press again. Remove the template and cut the fabric ⅛" from the second fold, so you have a finished stem with the 2 long edges pressed under. Make 30 stems.

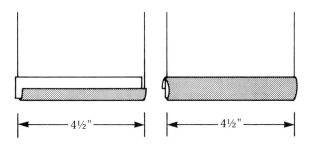

2. Trace the diagonal line on Template C on each background fabric square. To position the stem on each square, fold open the stem as shown, wrong side up, with the fold on the diagonal line. Machine stitch. Fold stem over seam and appliqué in place along folded edge. Trim excess.

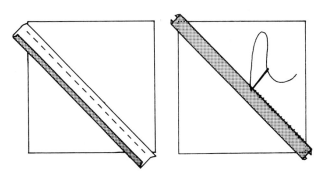

3. Appliqué 2 leaves onto each block. See Glossary (page 77) for paper-patch appliqué technique.

Ferol's Peony, 42" x 51", by Ferol Jess, 1902

Ferol in London, 45" x 45", by Gretchen Engle, Sharon Yenter, and Virginia Lauth

4. Piece blocks, following the piecing diagram.

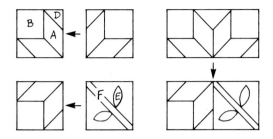

5. Sew lattice strips to Peony blocks and join into 6 rows of 5 blocks each.

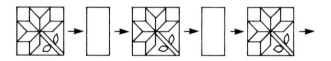

6. Beginning and ending with a lattice strip, join 5 lattice strips to 4 setting squares. Repeat with remaining strips and squares to make 5 horizontal rows.

7. Assemble rows of blocks with lattice rows between, referring to the quilt photo on page 46.
8. Add batting and backing, and quilt or tie. Bind edges with bias binding. See Glossary for finishing techniques.

Ferol in London

Quilt Photo: page 47

Quilt size: 45" x 45"
Block size: 6"

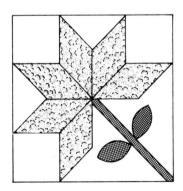

MATERIALS:
44"-WIDE FABRIC

¾ yd. print or assorted prints for peonies
1½ yds. background and lattice strips
½ yd. print or assorted prints for setting squares
½ yd. solid green for leaves and stems
½ yd. for center lattice strips
½ yd. for border
1 yd. for backing
½ yd. for binding

CUTTING

Use templates on pages 49 and 50.

1. Cut 96 of Template A from peony fabric or 6 for each block if you are using assorted prints.
2. Cut 48 of Template B, 16 of Template C, 96 of Template D, and 80 of Template H from background fabric.
3. Cut 25 of Template C from fabric(s) for setting squares.
4. Cut a strip of stem fabric, 4½" x 14", for stems.
5. Cut 32 leaves from Template E, adding a ¼"-wide seam allowance all around.
6. Cut 40 of Template H for center lattice strips.
7. Cut 4 pieces of border fabric, each 45" x 3½".

ASSEMBLY

1. Following the piecing instructions for Ferol's Peony, make 16 blocks.
2. Assemble 40 lattice strips as shown.

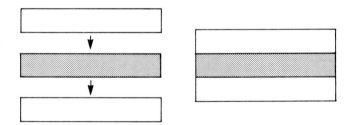

3. Following the diagram for step 5 of Ferol's Peony, sew lattice strips to Peony blocks, making 4 rows of 4 blocks each.
4. Beginning and ending with a setting square, join 4 lattice strips to 5 setting squares. Repeat with remaining strips and squares to make 5 horizontal rows.

5. Assemble rows of blocks and lattice rows, beginning and ending with a lattice row. Refer to quilt photo on page 51.
6. Sew borders to the 4 sides of the quilt. Miter the corners as shown in Glossary (page 76).
7. Add batting and backing, and quilt or tie. Bind edges with bias binding. See Glossary for finishing techniques.

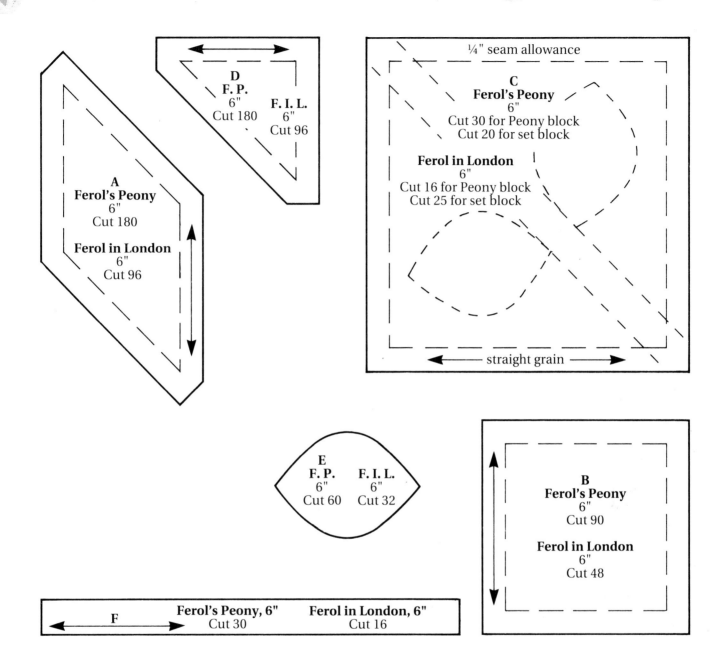

D
F. P.
6"
Cut 180

F. I. L.
6"
Cut 96

¼" seam allowance

C
Ferol's Peony
6"
Cut 30 for Peony block
Cut 20 for set block

Ferol in London
6"
Cut 16 for Peony block
Cut 25 for set block

straight grain

A
Ferol's Peony
6"
Cut 180

Ferol in London
6"
Cut 96

E
F. P.
6"
Cut 60

F. I. L.
6"
Cut 32

B
Ferol's Peony
6"
Cut 90

Ferol in London
6"
Cut 48

F

Ferol's Peony, 6"
Cut 30

Ferol in London, 6"
Cut 16

H
Ferol in London
6"
Cut 80 background
Cut 40 center lattice

straight grain

FROM OUR NEWSLETTER

QUILT PATTERN

By Cristel Hastings

NATURE *sewed the winter through,*
    Left-overs of gold and blue
From the sky . . . cerise and red
Stitched with white and silver thread.

PATIENTLY *she stitched along*
    To the north wind's lusty song . . .
Back and forth her needle flew
While the boist'rous March winds blew.

APRIL *dawned . . . the thing was done!*
    So she laid it in the sun.
Hills and gardens then were gay
With the patchwork quilt that lay . . .

BRIGHT, *and tufted deep with green,*
    Bordered with a brooklet's sheen . . .
Summer coverlet of scraps
Garnered from autumn's leafy wraps!

— *Needlecraft Magazine*
March, 1933

G
Ferol's Peony
6"
Cut 49

¼" seam allowance

Spring Baskets

Quilt Photos: page 53

TO MARKET, TO MARKET . . .

One of the nicest things about owning a shop is all the wonderful friends you make over the years—from customers to other shop owners. A favorite traveling companion of mine is Ann Stohl, who owned a store in Yakima, Washington. Ann and I have shared adventures around the country, but a most memorable occasion was a spring trip to Chicago for Quilt Market.

We arrived in Chicago at around 10 p.m., assuming that our guaranteed hotel reservations would be held for us. When we arrived at the desk, the young clerk informed us that there was "no room at the inn!" We immediately burst into tears (which works much better than anger). He took pity on us and said he had something for us after all.

He didn't have time to explain but he gave us a key, so we figured it must be a room and not the lobby. We opened the door . . . and found a huge party room with a fifteen-foot bar, sofas and chairs, screens, and a gorgeous view of Lake Michigan—but no beds or closet. After a few calls, we received a clothes rack on wheels and two rollaway beds. We were as cozy as two people in a ballroom! The next morning, we woke up feeling as if we had forgotten to go home after the party.

That evening we went to "Sample Spree," where we purchased store models of new patterns debuting at market. We bought dolls, bears, bunnies, and wall hangings galore. I had brought one of these basket wall hangings with me on the trip, and Ann had some quilts. We had great fun decorating our room. Every bear had a chair, the sofas were full of animals, and quilts brightened the walls. I'm sure the room had never been so comfy before the arrival of the "quiltie ladies."

This Spring Baskets pattern is designed to be used with any 8" quilt block that can be turned on point, or with squares of pictorial or theme fabrics. Instructions are given for a four-block and a six-block quilt.

Four-block quilt size: 36" x 36"
Six-block quilt size: 36" x 46"
Block size: 8"

MATERIALS:
44"- OR 54"-WIDE FABRIC

	4-block quilt	6-block quilt
Baskets	¼ yd. each of 4 different fabrics	¼ yd each of 3 different fabrics
Background for Basket Blocks	½ yd.	½ yd.
Setting Triangles and Inner Border	¾ yd.	¾ yd.
Middle Border	¼ yd.	¼ yd.
Outer Border	½ yd.	½ yd.
Backing	1¼ yds.	1½ yds.
Binding	½ yd.	½ yd.

CUTTING CHART
Use templates on page 55.

	4-block quilt	6-block quilt
From each Basket Fabric	1 of Template A 8 of Template E	2 of Template A 16 of Template E
Background for Basket Blocks	4 of Template A 4 of Template B 8 of Template C 4 of Template D 24 of Template E	6 of Template A 6 of Template B 12 of Template C 6 of Template D 36 of Template E
Setting Triangles and Squares	1 square, 8½" x 8½"	2 squares, each 8½" x 8½"
	1 square, 12⅝" x 12⅝; cut twice diagonally to make 4 side setting triangles	2 squares, each 12⅝" x 12⅝". Cut twice diagonally to make 8 side setting triangles. (You need only 6.)
	2 squares, each 6⅝" x ⅝"; cut once diagonally to make 4 corner setting triangles	2 squares, each 6⅝" x 6⅝"; cut once diagonally to make 4 corner setting triangles
Inner Border	4 strips, each 2½" x 35"	2 strips, each 2½" x 35" 2 strips, each 2½" x 44"
Middle Border	4 strips, each 1½" x 35"	2 strips, each 1½" x 35 2 strips, each 1½" x 44"
Outer Border	4 strips, each 3 1/2" x 37"	2 strips, each 3½" x 40" 3 strips, each 3½" wide; piece to make 2 strips, each 3½" x 50"

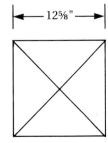

|← 12⅝" →|

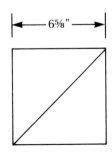

|← 6⅝" →|

Spring Baskets, 36" x 36", by Gretchen Engle

Spring Baskets, 36" x 46", by Gretchen Engle

ASSEMBLY

1. Piece Spring Basket blocks, following the piecing diagram. See Glossary (page 74) for machine-piecing techniques.

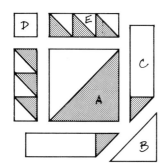

2. Assemble the pieced blocks, 8½" square(s), and side setting triangles into diagonal rows as shown. Sew the rows together, adding the 4 corner setting triangles. Refer to the quilt photo on page 53.

4-block quilt

6-block quilt

3. Piece 4 border sections, sewing an inner, middle, and outer border strip together for each side of the quilt.
4. Sew a border to each side of the quilt, mitering the corners as shown in the Glossary (page 74).
5. Add batting and backing, and quilt or tie. Bind the edges with bias binding. See Glossary for finishing techniques.

Sharon's top ten requirements for opening a quilt shop:

1. Cooperative family
2. House you can mortgage
3. Sense of humor
4. Love of fabric and quilts
5. Ability to work with people
6. Sense of humor
7. Good Scandinavian work ethic (even if you are Irish)
8. Constitution of a mule
9. Sense of humor
10. A second house plus a car, boat, kids, and husband you can mortgage.

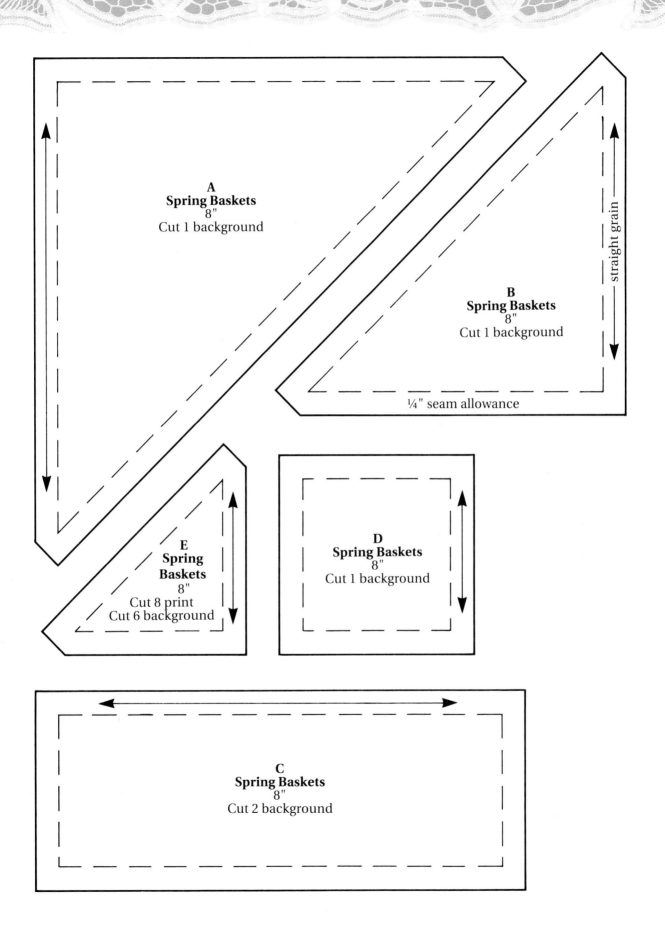

A
Spring Baskets
8"
Cut 1 background

B
Spring Baskets
8"
Cut 1 background

straight grain

¼" seam allowance

E
Spring Baskets
8"
Cut 8 print
Cut 6 background

D
Spring Baskets
8"
Cut 1 background

C
Spring Baskets
8"
Cut 2 background

English Village House

Jackie Quinn, one of our co-managers, made this wall hanging using a block drafted by our other co-manager, Kathleen Grady. Jackie taught this pattern at the store, and it was a popular class project. She is very familiar with houses because she has a lovely large family and swears she didn't get out of her house for twenty years. This experience makes her the perfect employee; she has developed many needlecraft skills and really enjoys coming to work!

Jackie used a large-flowered chintz with small pastel florals to achieve a sweet, whimsical look.

Quilt size: 40" x 44"
Block size: 14" x 16"

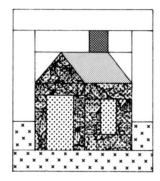

MATERIALS:
44"- OR 54"-WIDE FABRIC

Scraps of small and medium prints for houses, doors, and windows
Scraps of checks and plaids for roofs and chimneys
½ yd. flower print for gardens
1 yd. for background
½ yd. for sashing
⅔ yd. chintz for outer border
1¼ yds. for backing
½ yd. for binding

CUTTING

Use templates on pages 58, 59, 60, and 61.

1. From each of 4 house prints, cut 1 each of Templates E, G, H, and M. Cut 2 each of Templates I and K.
2. Cut 4 of Template B for chimneys, 4 of F for roofs, 4 of J for doors, and 4 of L for windows. Mix and match different fabrics; see the quilt photo on page 60 for ideas.
3. From the garden print fabric, cut 4 pieces, each 2½" x 14½", and 8 of Template N.
4. From the background fabric, cut:
   4 pieces, each 2½" x 14½"
   8 pieces, each 2½" x 9½"
   4 of Template A
   4 of Template C
   4 of Template D and 4 of D reversed
5. From the sashing fabric, cut:
   2 strips, each 1½" x 14½"
   3 strips, each 1½" x 33½"
   2 strips, each 1½" x 31½".
6. From the chintz, cut 2 strips, each 5" x 44", and 2 strips, each 5" x 40" across the width of the fabric.

ASSEMBLY

1. Piece 4 house blocks, following the piecing diagram.
   Note: When adding pieces D and D reversed to the roof, make sure that the short sides of the triangles lie at the top edge, not along the sides.

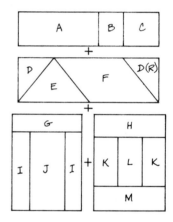

2. Sew a small garden-print piece (Template N) to one end of each of the 2½" x 9½" background pieces.
3. Sew a garden/background unit to both sides of each house, with the garden print at the bottom.
4. Sew 1 of the 4 remaining background strips to the top of each block, and 1 of the 4 garden-print strips to the bottom of each block.

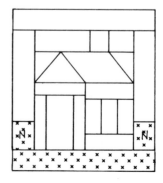

English Village House, 40" x 44", by Jackie Quinn

5. Measure the completed blocks. They should be 14½" x 16½". If they are not all the same size, trim the larger blocks to match the smallest. (If your blocks are smaller than 14½" x 16½", you will need to adjust the length of the sashing strips and chintz border strips.)

6. Lay the blocks out and move them around until you are happy with the placement.

7. Sew the short sashing strips between the top and bottom blocks.

8. Sew the 33½" sashing strips between the 2 pairs of blocks and to the 2 outside edges. Press seam allowances toward the sashing strips.

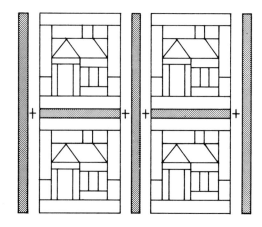

9. Sew the 31½" sashing strips to the top and bottom of the quilt. Press seam allowances toward the sashing strips.

10. Sew chintz border strips to the 4 sides of the quilt, mitering the corners as shown in the Glossary (page 74).

11. Add batting and backing, and quilt or tie. Bind edges with bias binding. See Glossary for finishing techniques.

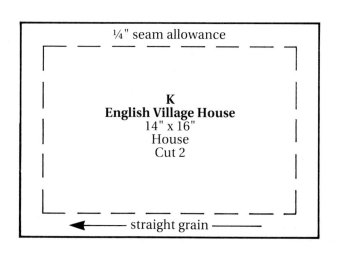

¼" seam allowance

K
English Village House
14" x 16"
House
Cut 2

◄──── straight grain ────

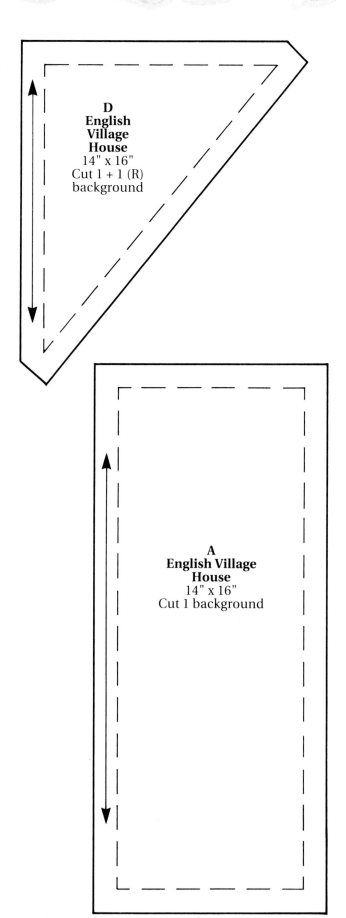

D
English Village House
14" x 16"
Cut 1 + 1 (R)
background

A
English Village House
14" x 16"
Cut 1 background

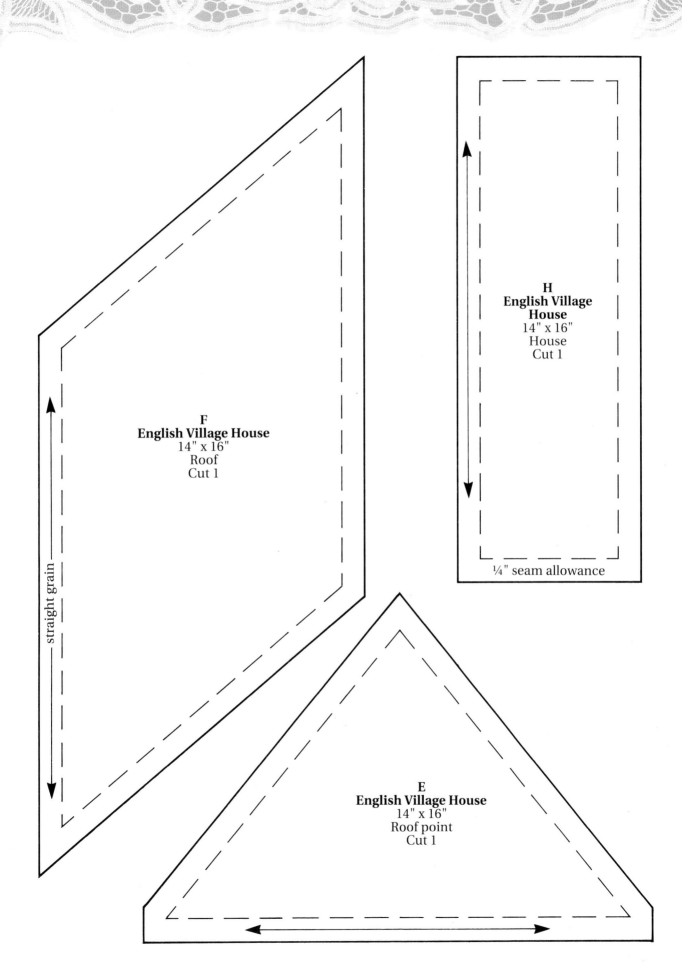

F
English Village House
14" x 16"
Roof
Cut 1

straight grain

H
English Village House
14" x 16"
House
Cut 1

¼" seam allowance

E
English Village House
14" x 16"
Roof point
Cut 1

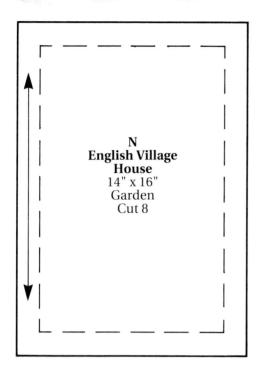

N
**English Village
House**
14" x 16"
Garden
Cut 8

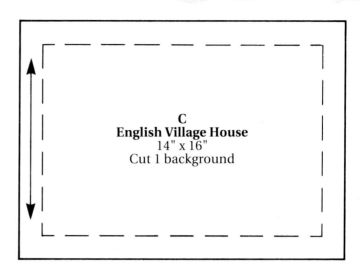

C
English Village House
14" x 16"
Cut 1 background

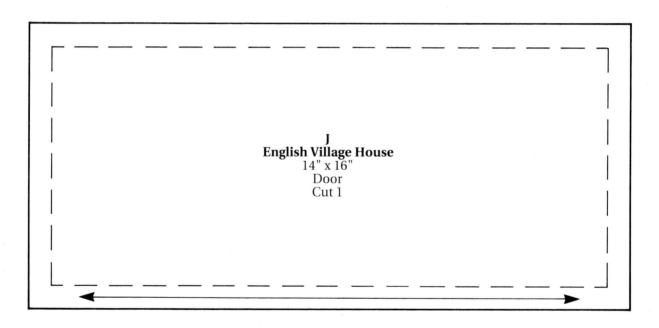

J
English Village House
14" x 16"
Door
Cut 1

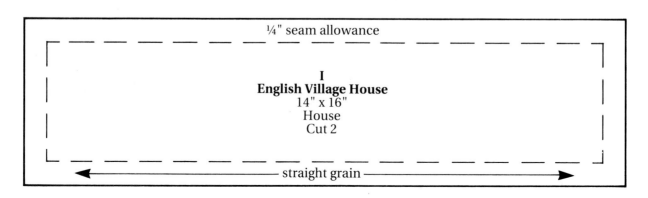

¼" seam allowance

I
English Village House
14" x 16"
House
Cut 2

straight grain

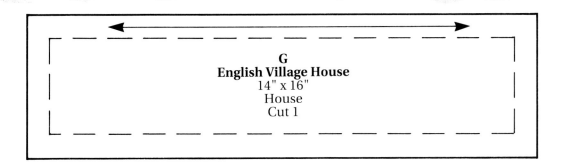

G
English Village House
14" x 16"
House
Cut 1

M
English Village House
14" x 16"
House
Cut 1

B
English Village House
14" x 16"
Chimney
Cut 1

¼" seam allowance

L
English Village House
14" x 16"
Window
Cut 4

straight grain

Cats in the Garden

Perfection is a worthy attribute, but perfect people aren't always as interesting and as much fun as others less perfect, and I feel the same way about quilts. When I started to sew this project, I realized I didn't have enough fabric to make four blocks with the same background, so I substituted and I like the effect much better.

Some of us may never master a Mariner's Compass or quilt eighteen stitches to the inch, but that doesn't mean our quilts can't be full of humor, whimsy, and personality. Some of the most valuable antique quilts are not technically perfect but are a delight because of the color, joy, and sense of adventure the quiltmaker instilled in her work.

Everything in life doesn't have to match. I once worked my booth at a quilt show for two days with mismatched shoes. Nobody noticed, not even me! At the end of a long show, we all had a badly needed laugh when I discovered why I was tilting slightly.

Lighten up—have some fun and let your personality come out! Don't anguish over small mistakes only you will notice. Quiltmaking is supposed to be fun.

Quilt size: 30" x 36"
Block size: 10" x 13"

MATERIALS:
44"- OR 54"-WIDE FABRIC

¼ yd. floral chintz for each cat, or ½ yd. if using the same fabric for all cats
Scraps for hearts
½ yd. for background
¼ yd. for lattice
Lace scraps for collars
⅝ yd. floral chintz for border
1 yd. for backing
½ yd. for binding

CUTTING
Use pattern pieces for cat found on pullout pattern insert.

1. From each cat fabric, cut 1 cat body, 1 cat head, and 2 cat tails.
2. Cut 2 hearts from scraps.
3. Cut 4 background pieces, each 10½" x 13½".
4. From lattice fabric, cut 2 strips, each 2½" x 10½", and 1 strip, 2½" x 28½".
5. From border fabric, cut 2 strips, each 4½" x 32", and 2 strips, each 4½" x 38".

ASSEMBLY

1. Appliqué hearts onto 2 cat bodies. See Glossary (page 77) for paper-patch appliqué instructions.
2. Prepare cat bodies for paper-patch appliqué.
3. With right sides together, stitch each pair of cat tails together, leaving short, straight end open. Clip and turn right side out. Stitch onto background fabric as shown.

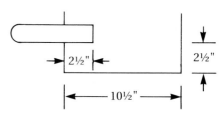

4. Appliqué cat bodies onto background pieces and over the tails as shown. Make sure you have 2 sets of cats facing each other. Do not stitch across the bottom of the cat. After appliquéing, take out the basting stitches and remove the paper from open bottom edge.

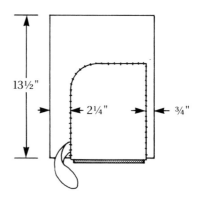

5. Assemble cat blocks and short lattice strips into 2 vertical rows. Sew the 2 rows to the long lattice strip as shown.

Cats in the Garden, 30" x 36", by Sharon Yenter and Virginia Lauth

6. Embroider the features on the cat faces, or draw them with a permanent pen. Appliqué the heads to the quilt, tipping them so that the ears touch across the lattice strip. Refer to the quilt photo above. Sew lace collars onto 2 cats.

7. Sew short border strips to top and bottom of the quilt, and long border strips to the sides. Miter the corners as shown in Glossary (page 74). Add batting or backing, and quilt or tie. Bind edges with bias binding. See Glossary for finishing techniques.

Garden Twist

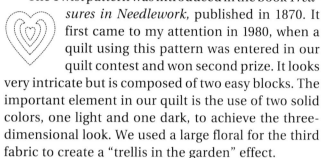

The Twist pattern was introduced in the book *Treasures in Needlework,* published in 1870. It first came to my attention in 1980, when a quilt using this pattern was entered in our quilt contest and won second prize. It looks very intricate but is composed of two easy blocks. The important element in our quilt is the use of two solid colors, one light and one dark, to achieve the three-dimensional look. We used a large floral for the third fabric to create a "trellis in the garden" effect.

Pay particular attention to the color layout to achieve the illusion of a lattice twining over a floral background.

Quilt size: 54" x 66"
Block size: 8"

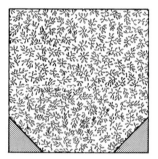

Floral A
Make 4
(2 with light triangles and
2 with dark triangles)

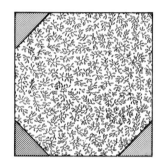

Floral B
Make 10
(5 with light triangles and
5 with dark triangles)

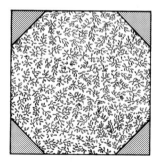

Floral C
Make 6
(3 with light triangles and
3 with dark triangles)

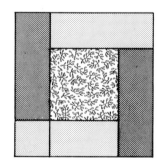

Alternate block
Make 12
(6 of each as shown in
piecing diagram at right)

MATERIALS:
44"- OR 54"-WIDE FABRIC

1½ yds. large floral print
¾ yd. light solid for trellis
¾ yd. dark solid for trellis
2 yds. for border
3¾ yds. for backing
½ yd. for binding

CUTTING

Use templates on pages 66, 67, and 68.

1. From the floral print, cut 20 of Template A. For Floral Block A, cut away 2 corners along the marked cutting line on 4 of these. For Floral Block B, cut away 3 corners on 10 of these in the same manner. For Floral Block C, cut away all 4 corners on the 6 remaining pieces. Cut 12 of Template C.
2. From both the light solid and the dark solid, cut:
   31 of Template B
   18 of Template D
   6 of Template E
   6 of Template F
3. From the border fabric, cut:
   14 large triangles, Template G
   4 small triangles, Template H
   2 strips, each 4½" x 60"
   2 strips, each 4½" x 72"

ASSEMBLY

1. Referring to the block diagrams above, piece:
   4 of Floral Block A, making 2 with light triangles and 2 with dark triangles.
   10 of Floral Block B, making 5 with light triangles and 5 with dark triangles.
   6 of Floral Block C, making 3 with light triangles and 3 with dark triangles.
2. Piece 12 alternate blocks, following the piecing diagram.

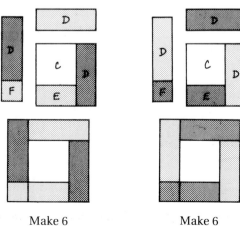

Make 6   Make 6

Garden Twist, 54" x 66", by Jackie Quinn and Michele Quinn

3. Sew the blocks together in diagonal rows as shown, adding the large setting triangles G to the sides and the small triangles H to the 4 corners. Refer to the quilt photo on page 65 to position the light and dark colors correctly.

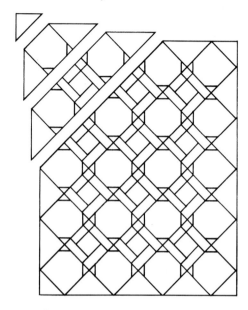

4. Add the border strips to the 4 sides of the quilt, mitering the corners as shown in Glossary (page 74).
5. Add batting and backing, and quilt or tie. Use outline quilting or quilting in the ditch around the trellis shape to create a three-dimensional illusion. Bind edges with bias binding. See Glossary for finishing techniques.

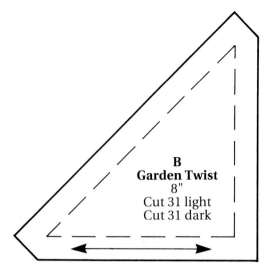

B
Garden Twist
8"
Cut 31 light
Cut 31 dark

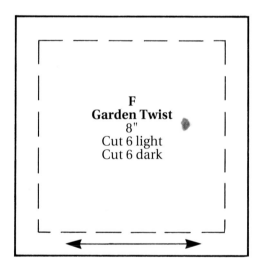

F
Garden Twist
8"
Cut 6 light
Cut 6 dark

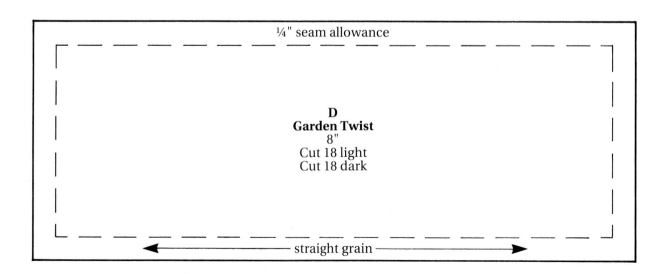

¼" seam allowance

D
Garden Twist
8"
Cut 18 light
Cut 18 dark

straight grain

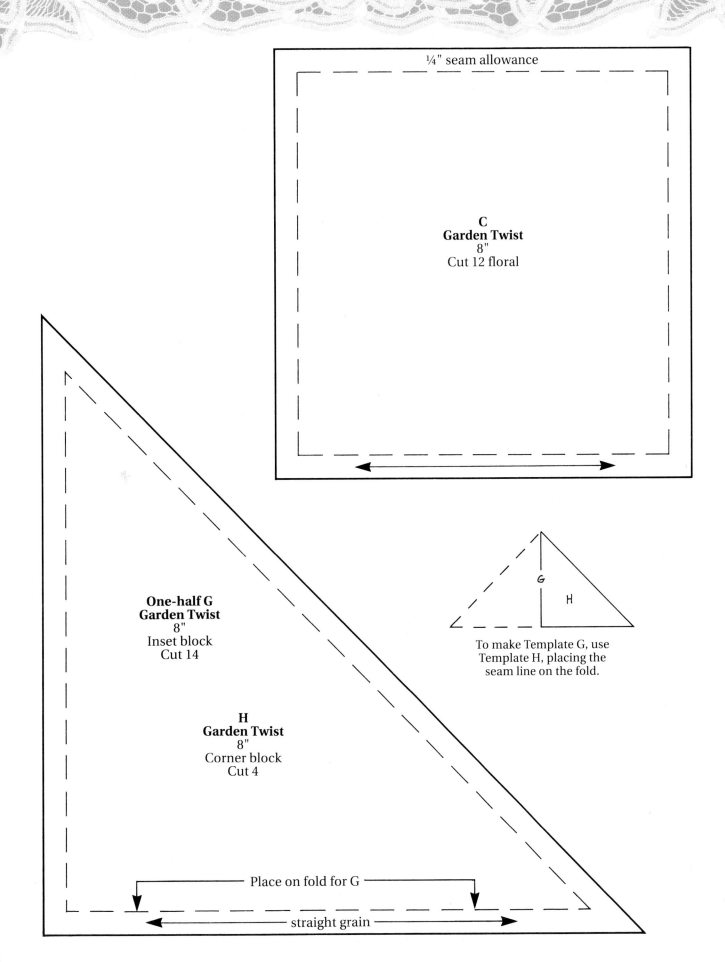

¼" seam allowance

C
Garden Twist
8"
Cut 12 floral

One-half G
Garden Twist
8"
Inset block
Cut 14

H
Garden Twist
8"
Corner block
Cut 4

G

H

To make Template G, use
Template H, placing the
seam line on the fold.

Place on fold for G

straight grain

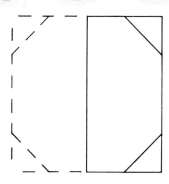

To make Template A, place
edge of half pattern on fold.

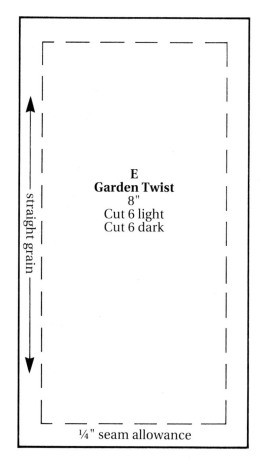

E
Garden Twist
8"
Cut 6 light
Cut 6 dark

straight grain

¼" seam allowance

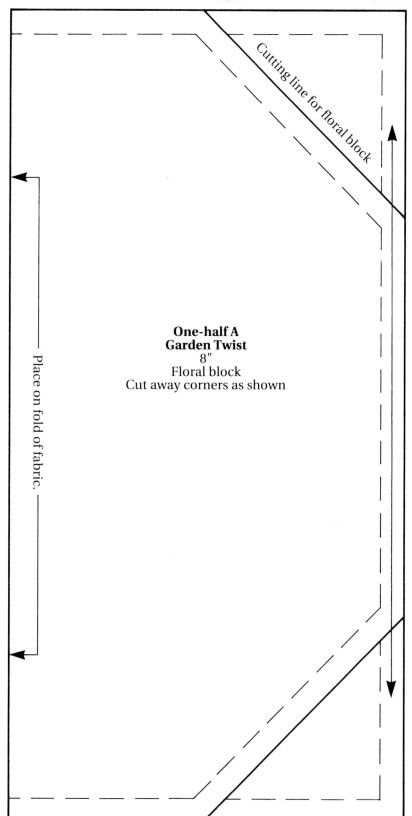

Cutting line for floral block

Place on fold of fabric.

One-half A
Garden Twist
8"
Floral block
Cut away corners as shown

Hidden Star
Quilt Photo: page 71

We thought of changing the name of Hidden Star to Hidden Inventory Star to memorialize that dreaded day when every item in the store must be counted. It's Cash for Stash Day, the day of reckoning, when staff members must claim and pay for all the little fabric hoards they've collected and hidden throughout the store all year. Everyone prays to win the lottery to pay the bill, but that hasn't happened yet. After the treasure has been ransomed, there's still the problem of getting it home, hiding it, and making it as unobtrusive as the stars in this quilt.

Over the years, we've discovered lots of creative ways to sneak fabric into our happy homes. A favorite was the staff member who saved small boxes and on Inventory Day arrived with a shopping bag full of Bisquick, cracker, and cake-mix boxes to fill with yards of fabric. This works well—unless you have an inquisitive husband who asks why there are ten boxes of Bisquick in the cupboard. Another employee keeps her treasures in plastic containers in the freezer because she has a husband who would never take the time to thaw anything. Both of these ideas might be the answer to the problem of adding more fiber to your diet!

Our saddest story involved the gal who kept all of her fabric in the trunk of her car. It was a smart idea until her car was stolen and then recovered, fabric intact. She and her husband had to go down to the police station and identify the contents. She was caught red-handed and had to admit that those ten boxes of fabric really did belong to her!

The Hidden Star quilt is a wonderful collage of color and geometric shapes. Arrange your fabric pieces so you barely see the stars, even though they are there.

Quilt size: 56½" x 56½"
Block size: 12"

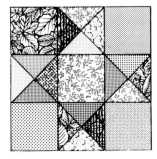

Block 1
Make 9

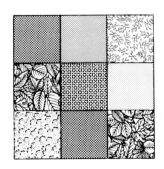

Block 2
Make 4

MATERIALS:
44"-WIDE FABRIC

2½ yds. assorted scraps for squares and stars, including some large chintz prints
1¼ yds. for background and binding
3½ yds. for backing

CUTTING
Use templates on page 72.
1. Cut 145 of Template A from a variety of fabrics.
2. Cut 144 of Template C from a variety of fabrics.
3. For outer-edge triangles, cut 4 of Template C and 36 of Template B from background fabric.

ASSEMBLY
1. Lay out squares (A) and triangles (C), following diagram. Move fabrics around until you are pleased with the arrangement.

2. Sew groups of 4 triangles together, then sew 4 triangle units to 5 squares to make each of 9 star blocks (Block 1).

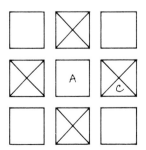

3. Sew 9 squares together to make each of the 4 Ninepatch blocks (Block 2) as shown.

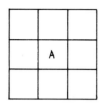

4. Sew 6 squares and 3 background triangles (C) together to make each of the 8 edge units.

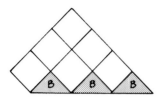

Make 4 like this   and 4 like this

5. Use 4 squares, 2 background triangles (C), and 1 background triangle (B) to make each of the 4 corner units. Add 2 more background triangles (C) to 2 of the units as shown.

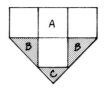 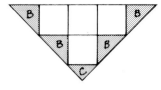

Make 2 like this   and 2 like this

6. Assemble the units into diagonal rows, referring to the quilt photo on page 72. Sew the rows together.

7. Add batting and backing, then quilt in zigzag lines as shown or tie. Bind edges with bias binding. See Glossary for finishing techniques.

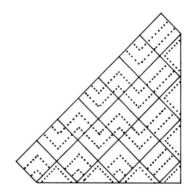

Hidden Star, 56½ " x 56½ ", by Gretchen Engle

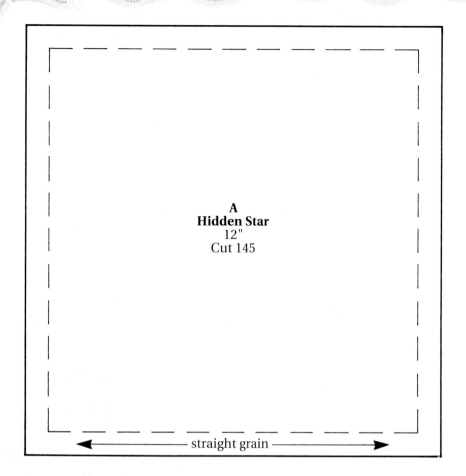

A
Hidden Star
12"
Cut 145

straight grain

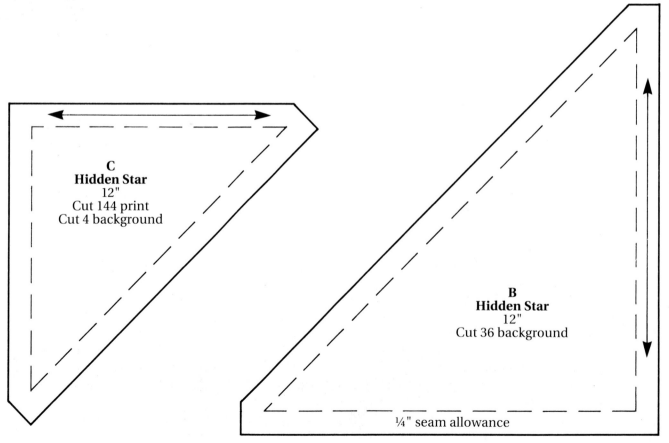

C
Hidden Star
12"
Cut 144 print
Cut 4 background

B
Hidden Star
12"
Cut 36 background

¼" seam allowance

It's easy to count all this fabric when you have energy food! Pictured from left: Jacquelyn Kerrigan, Ben Yenter, Jason Yenter, Cathy Miller, Florence Evans, Bill Yenter, Sharon Evans Yenter

Inventory Eats

The best thing about Inventory Day is the potluck we have at lunchtime. We require that the dishes staff members bring to share take no longer than ten minutes to prepare. Here are two of the staff's favorites.

FLORENCE'S TANGY CHICKEN

1 10-oz. can jellied cranberry sauce
1 8-oz. bottle sweet and spicy French dressing
1 envelope dry onion soup mix
2–3 lbs. boneless chicken breast

Preheat oven to 325°F. Mix cranberry sauce, French dressing, and soup mix in blender. Pour over chicken pieces in casserole dish. Cover and bake approximately 1 hour, until tender. Serves 4 to 6.

INVENTORY BEANS

Contributed by Jean Bergersen. (No, you don't have to count the beans before you make this.)

1 lb. hamburger
4 15-oz. cans kidney beans, drained (or mix different kinds of beans)
¼ c. molasses
¼ c. vinegar
½ c. brown sugar
1 T. prepared mustard
¼ c. catsup
¼ t. salt
1 envelope dry onion soup mix

Preheat over to 350°F. Brown hamburger, then add beans. Mix all other ingredients together and stir to blend. Pour into hamburger-bean mixture. Bake in a covered casserole dish for 1 hour. Serves 6 to 8.

Glossary

THREAD

For machine piecing, use white or neutral thread as light in color as your lightest fabric. Use dark neutral thread for piecing dark solids. One hundred percent cotton thread is easier to work with on some machines. For hand quilting, use special quilting thread, or wax your regular thread. Sport-weight yarn or pearl cotton for tying works well.

MACHINE PIECING

Sew exact ¼"-wide seams. To determine the ¼" seam allowance on your machine, place a template under the presser foot and gently lower the needle onto the seam line. The distance from the needle to the edge of the template is ¼". Lay a piece of masking tape at the edge of the template to act as the ¼" guide. If the presser foot edge is at the ¼" mark, use the edge as a guide. Set the stitch length at 10 to 12 stitches per inch. Backtack if you wish, although it is not really necessary, as each seam will be crossed and held by another.

Use chain piecing whenever possible to save time and thread. To chain piece, sew one seam, but do not lift the presser foot. Do not take the piece out of the sewing machine and do not cut the thread. Instead, set up the next seam to be sewn and stitch it as you did the first. There will be a little twist of thread between the two pieces. Sew all the seams you can at one time in this way, then remove the "chain." Clip the threads.

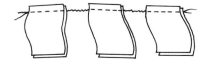

Press the seam allowances to one side, toward the darker fabric whenever possible. Avoid too much pressing as you sew because it tends to stretch bias grains and distort fabric shapes.

To piece a unit block, sew the smallest pieces together first to form units. Join smaller units to form larger ones until the block is complete. Pay close attention to the design, the drawing, and the sewing instructions given with each pattern.

Short seams do not require pinning unless matching is involved, or the seam is longer than 4". Keep pins away from the seam line. Sewing over pins tends to burr the needle and makes it difficult to be accurate in tight places.

Ideally, if pieces are cut and sewn precisely, patchwork designs will come out flat and smooth with crisply matched corners and points. In practice, it doesn't always happen that way. Here are four matching techniques that can be helpful in many different piecing situations.

1. **Opposing seams.** When stitching one seamed unit to another, press seam allowances on the seams that need to match, in opposite directions. The two "opposing" seams will hold each other in place and evenly distribute the bulk. Plan pressing to take advantage of opposing seams.

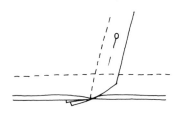

2. **Positioning pin.** Push a pin carefully straight through two points that must be matched and pull the two pieces tightly together. With the positioning pin in place, pin the seam normally and then remove the positioning pin.

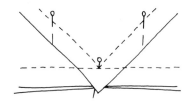

3. **The X.** When triangles are pieced, stitches form an X at the next seam line. Stitch through the center of the X to avoid chopping off the points on the sewn triangles.

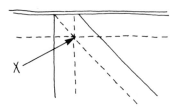

4. **Easing.** When two pieces to be sewn together are supposed to match but instead are slightly different lengths, pin the points of matching and stitch with the shorter piece on top. The feed dogs will ease in the fullness of the bottom piece as you stitch.

It is possible to do beautiful and accurate piecing with a sewing machine.

Try to correct mistakes when they happen—keep a seam ripper handy—but don't spend too much time ripping out and restitching. Some sewing inaccuracies can be corrected, others cannot. Sometimes the best thing is to move on and make the next block better. The quality of your piecing will improve with each block you piece.

ATTACHING BORDERS WITH MITERED CORNERS

1. Prepare the border strips. Determine the finished outside dimensions of your quilt (finished quilt-top dimensions *and* finished width of border). Cut the borders this length plus ½" for seam allowances.

    Sew multiple borders together and treat the resulting "striped" units as a single border for mitering.

    Note: When using striped fabric, make sure the design on all four borders is cut the same way.

2. To attach the borders to the pieced section of the quilt, center each border on a side so the ends extend equally on either side of the center section. Using a ¼"-wide seam allowance, sew the border to quilt top, leaving ¼" unsewn at the beginning and end of the stitching line. Backstitch at each end. Press the seam allowance toward border.

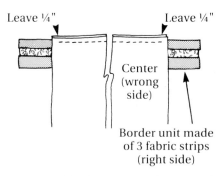

3. Arrange the first corner to be mitered on the ironing board as shown.

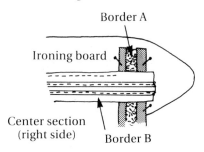

Press it flat and straight. To prevent it from slipping, pin the quilt to the ironing board. Turn border B right side up and fold under the corner to be mitered at a 45° angle. Match the raw edges underneath with those of border A. Any stripes and border designs should meet. Check the squareness of the corner with a right angle. Press the fold. This will be the sewing line.

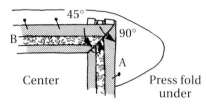

Pin the borders together to prevent shifting and unpin the piece to remove it from the ironing board. Turn wrong side out and pin along fold line, readjusting if necessary to match designs (and seam lines in a pieced border).

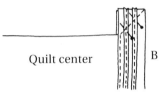

4. Machine baste from the inside to the outside corner on the fold line, leaving ¼" at the beginning unsewn. Check for accuracy. If it's right, sew again with regular stitch. Backstitch at the beginning and end of the stitching. (After you've done mitered corners several times, the basting step won't be necessary.) Trim away excess fabric, leaving a ¼" allowance along the mitered seam. Press open. Press the other seams to the outside.

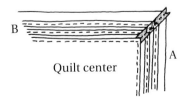

MARKING THE QUILTING DESIGN

Press the completed quilt top and mark quilting designs. Choose one of these methods.

1. **Commercial stencil designs.** These may be traced on with a water-soluble marking pen. Mark with dots rather than a solid line so that the marks will be easier to remove. Before you mark the quilt top, test the marker on a piece of the fabric used in your quilt. Wash the marks out with cold water. Do not press the fabric after marking it, or put the quilt through the clothes dryer, until you are certain you have removed all of the marks. Heat can set the marks permanently.

2. **Quilting in the ditch** (quilting in the seam lines). If you quilt along seam lines, you do not have to mark the quilting lines. If you plan to quilt in the ditch, press all seams in the direction away from where you plan to quilt.

3. **Quilting around the design** (¼" away). You may not need to mark the quilting lines if you can "eyeball" this distance. Masking tape ¼" wide is available for marking quilts for ¼" quilting. Place the tape on your quilt top along the seam line and stitch close to the edge, then remove the tape.

BACKING

The construction of the backing is very important to the quality of your finished quilt. Don't try to skimp here by using inexpensive fabric or by piecing incorrectly. Remember the time and thought that went into the top.

Quilt show judges consider the back of a quilt when scoring; even though you may not be entering a competition, you should take pride in your entire piece.

After you wash and press the backing fabric, you should have about 42" of usable cloth from the original 45" width. Buy enough fabric to allow at least 3" of backing to extend all around the outer edge of the quilt top, before washing. Cut off selvages.

A single length of 45"-wide fabric is often adequate for small projects. For larger quilts, you must seam two or three pieces of fabric together to make a back. Do not place a seam down the center of the quilt backing. Use one complete width of your fabric in the center and cut the other width in half lengthwise. Sew one half to each long side of the center panel. Press seams open.

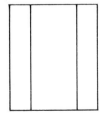

Alternatively, you can sew three widths of fabric together to make a backing for a large quilt.

If you are only a few inches short and do not want to buy another length of fabric, consider adding a border to the back; it can be an attractive design feature. Calculate the number of inches you need to add and sew border strips of equal widths to all four sides of the back.

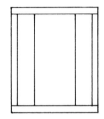

A third choice is to piece the back, making a two-sided quilt. One fun and creative approach would be to utilize scraps from the quilt top to make a pieced design of large squares, triangles, or rectangles.

BATTING

Batting is very important to the finished appearance of your quilt. Batting that is too thick and puffy has been the downfall of many an otherwise successful quilt or wall hanging. Use thick batting only when you plan to tie the quilt.

I prefer prepackaged batting because batting sturdy enough to be sold on bolts is invariably too thick or uneven for hand or machine quilting. Companies now produce many thicknesses of batting. Ask your quilt-store salesperson to explain the differences.

Most 100% cotton batting must be quilted very densely or it will shift, and stitching through the cotton is difficult. A batting that is 80% cotton and 20% polyester may be a better choice; it is quite flat but still requires fairly dense quilting.

Batting of 100% polyester is available in a variety of thicknesses and bed sizes. It works very well for most projects. One of the newest polyester batts is Low Loft, which is excellent for hand and machine quilting. (Ask for a "Low Life" batt, as one of our customers did recently, and we'll still know what you mean!) I prefer a bonded batt because the bonding helps prevent the migration of fibers, those pesky little pieces of batting that want to come through the surface of a quilt.

When in doubt, purchase a low-loft or lightweight bonded batt. Your quilt will be warm enough, and your stitches will look lovely. You can also use it for wall hangings, or you may want to try a heavyweight-cotton shirting flannel.

BASTING THE QUILT LAYERS

Spread out the quilt backing on the floor or a large table, right side down. Cover with your batt, then center the quilt on top. Smooth the top so it lies flat. Starting in the center, make diagonal, vertical, and horizontal rows of basting stitches, spacing them about 8" apart.

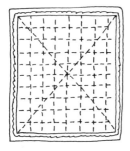

An alternative method is pin basting with size 2 rustproof safety pins, which are available in bulk at most quilt stores. You will need about 500 safety pins to baste a queen-size quilt.

QUILTING

There are several ways to finish your quilt. Machine quilting has become increasingly popular in the last few years, and several books are devoted entirely to this technique. Large commercial quilting machines are popular, and it is quite easy now to find a business to quilt your top.

If you want to take the time to create an heirloom, I recommend the old hand-quilting methods. Hand quilting takes practice, so don't be discouraged if your first stitches are not as small and even as you'd like them to be. Try to keep your stitches even and don't worry too much about the size.

Most brands of quilting thread will work well, whether 100% cotton or cotton-covered polyester. Cut your thread about 18" long and make a small knot in one end. Quilting needles called "betweens" or "hand-quilting needles" are available in sizes 6 through 12, with 12 being the finest. (The larger the number, the finer the needle.) Use the smallest size you are able to thread and use comfortably. For beginners, this is usually an 8 or 9.

You will probably want to wear a thimble on the middle finger of your quilting hand. It may be difficult to get used to at first, but it is very necessary—to prevent sore and bleeding fingers.

To quilt, insert the needle into the quilt top and batting. Pull sharply so the knot becomes imbedded in the batt. Make small running stitches through all three layers, using the thimble to push the needle through. When you are close to the end of the thread, wind it twice around the needle and stab the needle through the top and the batting. Pull the thread to bury the knot in the batting. Bring the thread to the surface and snip it off.

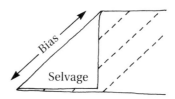

BIAS BINDING

Encasing raw edges in bias binding is an attractive and convenient way to finish many projects. It's easy to make your own bias binding. I prefer double-folded bias binding because it wears better. The directions that follow are for this type of binding.

1. Fold over a corner of fabric to find the true bias. Make a crease at the fold.

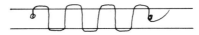

2. Open the fold and cut along the crease. Measure and mark strips the width you need, including seam allowances. Cut along the marked lines.

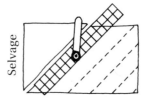

3. With right sides together, machine stitch the bias strips together, end to end, to make one long strip. Press seams open.

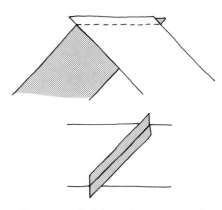

4. Cut one end of the strip at a 45° angle. Turn under ¼" and press.

5. Fold the strip in half, wrong sides together, and press a crease down the center, being careful not to stretch the bias.

6. Place the raw edges of the folded bias even with the unfinished edge on the right side of the quilt in the center of one side. Machine stitch ¼" from raw edges of the bias, stopping ¼" from the corner. Backstitch. Remove from the machine.

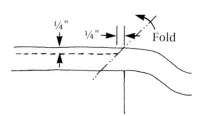

7. On the next side, fold the binding away from the quilt and then down so it is even with the next side and the fold at the top is parallel to the quilt edge. Stitch from the edge to the next corner, ending stitching ¼" from the corner as in step 6, above. Continue on remaining sides of quilt.

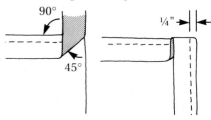

8. When you reach the beginning of the binding, overlap the stitching about 1" and trim the end of the binding, tucking it into the fold as shown.

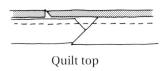

Quilt top

9. Turn the folded edge of the bias binding over the raw edges so that the stitching line is not visible on the back side of the quilt. Using matching thread, hand sew the binding in place on the back side of the quilt.

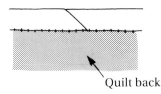

Quilt back

CONTINUOUS BIAS BINDING

This is a good technique for finishing a quilt or large project, because it eliminates sewing many small seams to join short bias strips into one long strip.

An 18" square will make 3½ yards of 2"-wide bias. A half-yard piece of fabric, cut into two squares, will make 7 yards. You can make enough bias for most large quilts from ¾ to 1 yard of fabric.

1. Begin with a square of fabric. Fold diagonally and press. With a pencil, mark the centers of the opposite sides of the square. Cut along the diagonal line.

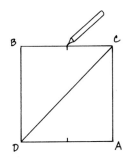

2. With right sides together and pencil marks matching, stitch the two triangles together and press the seam open.

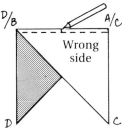

Wrong side

3. Draw pencil lines spaced the width of your unfinished bias strips between D/B-C and A/C-D on the wrong side of the fabric. These will be your cutting lines.

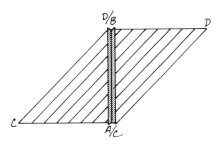

4. Pin point D/B to the first pencil line in from point C with right sides together. Match remaining pencil lines and pin, creating a lopsided tube.

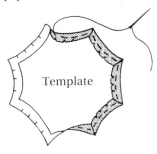

5. Sew the seam and press open. Starting at D/B, cut around the tube on the pencil lines for yards of continuous bias.

APPLIQUÉ

Preparing the block. When constructing an appliqué block, the resulting block will be accurate if you draw the pattern onto the background fabric before placing the appliqué pieces on the fabric.

1. Draw the pattern on a large piece of newsprint or graph paper. (If necessary, tape smaller pieces of paper together). Make the pattern the size of the finished block plus a ¼"-wide seam allowance all around.
2. Fold the paper block diagonally, horizontally, and vertically to help with placement. Transfer the appliqué pattern onto the paper, one quarter of the block at a time.
3. Place the background fabric over the paper block and trace the pattern onto the fabric, using a hard lead pencil. An easy way to do this is to tape the fabric and paper to a window or place them on a glass coffee table with a flashlight underneath. The light coming from behind the paper will make the pencil lines clearly visible, so you can easily trace the design.

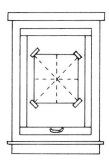

Paper-Patch Appliqué: Make a paper template of each appliqué shape without seam allowance. Inexpensive materials for this include old Christmas or greeting cards or those irritating advertising pullouts in magazines.

1. Pin the paper patches to the wrong side of the appliqué fabric. Pin from the right side of the fabric to prevent the thread from catching as you baste from the wrong side. Cut out the appliqué shapes, adding a ¼"-wide seam allowance all around.
2. Turn the seam allowance over onto the paper and baste.

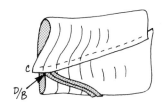

Template

Note: Clip the seam allowance on curves and sharp dips.

Points, such as the tips of leaves, should be folded over the top of the paper patch. Fold one side over and trim. Fold the other side over and baste.

Template

For circles, cut the fabric using your circle paper-patch template as a guide, then remove the paper-patch. Run a row of basting stitches around the outer edge of the circle fabric. Pull the thread and gather carefully. Replace the paper patch and gather tightly. Baste the template to the fabric.

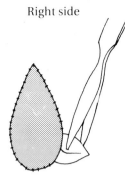

Right side

3. After basting, lightly press only the folded edges. (The basting stitches may make indentations in the finished appliqué if you press over them.)

4. Place the prepared appliqué shapes on the background fabric. Use a long machine-basting stitch or pin the appliqué shapes onto the background fabric to hold them in place. Permanently hand stitch the shapes in place in numerical order as marked on the templates. Use a blind hem stitch, spacing the stitches evenly, 1/16" to 1/8" apart. Pieces that must fit under other pieces must be sewn in place first. Match your thread to each appliqué shape.

5. After all shapes have been stitched to the background fabric, remove the basting threads. Turn the block over to the wrong side and cut through the background fabric only to remove the paper templates. You can cut only a small slit, or you can trim the background away almost to the stitching line. The second method reduces bulk but makes the block more fragile.

Wrong side

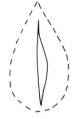 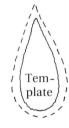

If you prefer not to cut into the back of your block, stitch around the appliqué shape but leave 1/2" unstitched. Remove the basting stitches. Using tweezers, pull the paper template out from inside the appliqué. Close the opening with blind hem stitching.

Appliqué Stems. Bias strips are used for narrow curving pieces, such as stems. To find the true bias of your fabric, fold it diagonally until you find the most stretch. On uncut fabric, the selvages will be parallel. After cutting diagonal strips of the length and width required, choose one of the following methods to make the bias stems.

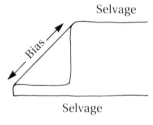

The first method requires a double thickness of fabric, so it makes a bulky stem, but it is the most appropriate technique for long stems. The second method is less bulky.

Method One: Cut a piece of bias twice the finished width of the stem plus a 1/4"-wide seam allowance for each edge. Fold in half, wrong sides together, and press. Place the 1/4" seam line of the open edge of bias on the outside penciled line of the stem as shown. Machine stitch on the seam line.

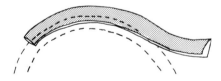

Trim the top seam allowance of the stem narrower than the bottom one to grade them and reduce bulk. Then fold the bias piece to the inside penciled stem line and blindstitch in place.

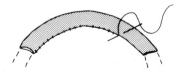

Method Two. Make a template the finished width and length of the stem. This can be made from cardstock or old manila file folders. Cut a piece of bias the finished width of the stem plus a 1/4"-wide seam allowance on each edge. Place the fabric on your ironing board, right side down. Center the template on the fabric.

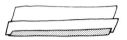

Press one side of the fabric over the template and then the other. Remove the template. Place the folded edges of the stem on the penciled placement lines on the background fabric. Blindstitch or machine stitch in place, starting with the outer edge.

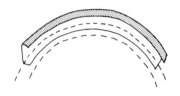

In the Beginning . . .

I've had a wonderful fifteen years running my store. A person is truly blessed when their passion is their work. It's been a long road from mortgaging our house and working years without pay to the present In the Beginning, one of the largest quilt shops in the United States.

If opening a quilt shop is your dream, I strongly recommend that you follow that dream with the understanding that you might have a few nightmares along the way! I've met wonderful people, had grand experiences, and worked harder than I've worked at any other time in my life. The rewards are many, and while you might not have time to do a lot of your own quilting, you'll have the pleasure of seeing other people progress because of your interest.

Shop owners are caretakers of the tradition of quiltmaking. They keep the enthusiasm alive by offering classes and exciting fabrics and products, by spotting innovative techniques, and by generally creating a colorful, happy atmosphere in which quilters can converge.

I'm proud to be a participant in the great quilt movement of the 1970s, '80s, and '90s, and I hope the legacy continues into the next century.

Support your local quilt shop—it's a habit worth supporting.

Sharon Evans Yenter

Many of the fabrics and quilt notions featured in this book are available at your local quilt shop. If you are unable to find specific items, write to us or phone In the Beginning Fabrics. Our mail-order specialist will be happy to help you.

In the Beginning Fabrics
8201 Lake City Way NE
Seattle, Washington 98115
(206) 523-1121

THAT PATCHWORK PLACE PUBLICATIONS AND PRODUCTS

The Americana Collection by Nancy Southerland-Holmes
    Liberty Eagle
    Old Glory
    Stars and Stripes
    Uncle Sam
Angelsong by Joan Vibert
Angle Antics by Mary Hickey
Appliqué Borders: An Added Grace by Jeana Kimball
Baby Quilts from Grandma by Carolann M. Palmer
Back to Square One by Nancy J. Martin
A Banner Year by Nancy J. Martin
Basket Garden by Mary Hickey
Blockbuster Quilts by Margaret J. Miller
Calendar Quilts by Joan Hanson
Cathedral Window: A Fresh Look by Nancy J. Martin
Copy Art for Quilters by Nancy J. Martin
Country Threads by Connie Tesene and Mary Tendall
Even More by Trudie Hughes
Fantasy Flowers: Pieced Flowers for Quilters
    by Doreen Cronkite Burbank
Feathered Star Sampler by Marsha McCloskey
Fit To Be Tied by Judy Hopkins
Five- and Seven-Patch Blocks & Quilts for the
    ScrapSaver™ by Judy Hopkins
Four-Patch Blocks & Quilts for the ScrapSaver™
    by Judy Hopkins
Handmade Quilts by Mimi Dietrich
Happy Endings—Finishing the Edges of Your Quilt
    by Mimi Dietrich
Holiday Happenings by Christal Carter
Home for Christmas by Nancy J. Martin and
    Sharon Stanley
Lessons in Machine Piecing by Marsha McCloskey
Little By Little: Quilts in Miniature by Mary Hickey
More Template-Free™ *Quiltmaking* by Trudie Hughes
My Mother's Quilts: Designs from the Thirties by
    Sara Nephew
Nifty Ninepatches by Carolann M. Palmer
Nine-Patch Blocks & Quilts for the ScrapSaver™
    by Judy Hopkins
Not Just Quilts by Jo Parrott
Ocean Waves by Marsha McCloskey and Nancy J. Martin
One-of-a-Kind Quilts by Judy Hopkins
Pineapple Passion by Nancy Smith and Lynda Milligan
Quilts to Share by Janet Kime
Red and Green: An Appliqué Tradition by Jeana Kimball
Reflections of Baltimore by Jeana Kimball
Rotary Riot: 40 Fast and Fabulous Quilts by Judy Hopkins
    and Nancy J. Martin
Scrap Happy by Sally Schneider
Shortcuts: A Concise Guide to Metric Rotary Cutting
    by Donna Lynn Thomas
Shortcuts: A Concise Guide to Rotary Cutting
    by Donna Lynn Thomas
Small Talk by Donna Lynn Thomas
Stars and Stepping Stones by Marsha McCloskey
Tea Party Time: Romantic Quilts and Tasty Tidbits
    by Nancy J. Martin
Template-Free™ *Quiltmaking* by Trudie Hughes
Template-Free™ *Quilts and Borders* by Trudie Hughes
Threads of Time by Nancy J. Martin
Women and Their Quilts by Nancyann Johanson Twelker

Tools
6" Bias Square®
8" Bias Square®
Metric Bias Square®
BiRangle™
Pineapple Rule
Rotary Mate™
Rotary Rule™
ScrapSaver™

Video
Shortcuts to America's
Best-Loved Quilts

Many titles are available at your local quilt shop. For more information, send $2 for a color catalog to That Patchwork Place, Inc., PO Box 118, Bothell WA 98041-0118.